The Perception Transformation Collection:

How to See and Think Differently

Chris Smythe

The Perception Transformation

How to transform the reality by understanding our perception

Chris Smythe

Contents

Introduction

How do you know what you see is real? Well, quite simply put, you do not. Your mind tells you that what you see is in fact real, but there is no way to prove it. With respect to those around you, there is no way to be sure if you see, or rather 'perceive', the same things that they do.

The point being made here is that even if your senses receive something, a certain sight, sound or smell, how can you tell if it is real if others do not sense the same thing? Well, actually they do. But they 'perceive' it differently. What does that mean? Perception is different from sight. It is on a different level from our senses and it, ultimately, shapes our reality. It tells our mind what we see and what we hear.

When our senses gather information from the world, it is really in the form of facts. A sight we see is a combination of colors, a mixture of light and darkness. Smells and sounds are vibrational and molecular signals carried by the air to our nose and ears. The surface texture and feel of a particular object is a sensory signal which is transmitted by our nerves to the brain, and particular signals which come in contact with our tongue are received as taste.

But after these signals have been received, the senses are no longer important. What becomes important, is our perception. The sensory signals are interpreted by our mind, based on our memories, knowledge and our understanding of the world around us from past experiences. The information our senses give us is translated into something meaningful, something which we understand and something which triggers our emotions.

It can sometimes be difficult to understand the true meaning of perception. One would first have to understand the meaning of reality. Debates in Experimental psychology have aimed to answer these questions, but here we take a much simpler approach. Reality is the state of things as they actually exist. That is, of course, in the present state. Or you could say, at the time at which our senses gather information.

But since the information which our senses send to our brain, is altered and manipulated in a way which we fail to understand, what we see as our reality is actually our perception of the world, and not the world as it actually is. This is not to say that what we see is completely different from what others see. It simply means that each person sees the world slightly differently from what it actually is and from how others see it as well.

Perception is a powerful force. It affects everything in our reality and, in fact, it constantly changes our reality as we go through experiences in life. Emotions are what follows perception, and they could be negative or positive. Experiences give rise to memories, which give rise to emotions, which change our perception, and this changes our emotions again. And so, a dynamic cycle of how our perception influences our reality is put into place from the moment we begin to experience life as sentient beings.

Now that we have established a definition of reality and seen how it is affected by our experiences, we can start to take a closer look at perception. It is useful to learn some basic terms which psychologists use. The object, sight, sound or smell etc., which our senses detect is called *distal stimulus* or *distal object*. Our senses then transform the detection of this stimulus into a neural signal, through a process known as *transduction*. The neural activity is called the *proximal stimulus*, and once the brain receives the neural signals, it recreates the *distal stimulus* in the sub-conscience. The process through which the brain does this is called *precept*, and the resulting reconstructed images are known as Perception.

Consider a man crossing a road. A brightly colored car approaches swiftly from one side, honking its horn as it comes towards the person. The person sees the car, and hears the horn. He moves aside to let the car pass, instead of trying to cross the road.

In this case, the car is the stimulus. The light reflected off the car, and the sound of the horn, are detected by the person's senses of sight and sound, respectively. They are then converted into neural signals, called the proximal stimulus, and transmitted to the brain, through transduction. The brain recreates the image of the car in the person's mind, and his memory and experience tells him he should move aside or the car will hit him and so he does. This is perception.

Of course, perception is affected by opinions. Our experiences in life are either pleasant or unpleasant. Experiences affect emotions, and since emotions affect perception, our perception mold's our opinions about certain situations, people, objects, and of course sights and sounds. The process of forming opinions is described by psychologists as follows:

- We encounter a previously un-encountered situation.

- There are no experiences and no memories which can drastically affect our perception, but we do have certain informational cues.

- As curious creatures, we want to learn more about the subject.

- As we try to gather information and learn, we recognize certain familiar informational signals, which allow us to classify the subject.

- Finally, we become adamant in the way our classification process progresses. Any information, or signals which go against our initial recognition, is immediately ignored, and more cues related to the same classification strengthen our theory. An image or opinion is formed.

Once an opinion is formed, we carry it with us for a very long time. We view the world through the lens of our experiences. Furthermore, opinions continue to influence perception, until substantial compelling evidence is presented to us which completely shatters our initial opinion. And, of course, since everyone has different experiences in life, they have different opinions, and thus, different perceptions of the same things.

The same subject (or stimulus) can be perceived by various people, differently. Again, this traces back to their experiences. It can also be linked to people's knowledge, beliefs, and their expectations. It is also linked to their efforts and motivations. This concept is explored in much greater detail in Chapter 2, but we will touch on it here as well.

Consider a person who lost a loved one due to a complication during heart surgery. When someone else close to him develops a similar illness, which forces them to undergo heart surgery as well, the person's perception of his past experience comes into effect. He may view the surgery as a risky and complicated procedure. He may even discourage his loved one from undergoing such a treatment.

Before he lost someone close to him, perhaps he believed that surgery was a good option and that a medical procedure would improve their standard of living. But instead, in his case, it made matters worse. He feels let down, and thus his opinions on heart surgery have completely changed. If the person, who needs the surgery now, actually improves his health after the procedure, this may slightly change the opinion of the person under scrutiny here. This would also be an example of how drastic events can sometimes change our perception. Then again, that depends entirely on the person and his/her obstinacy.

Social guidelines such as justice, equality, kindness, and vendetta, are also very important in shaping our perceptions. The two most important theories which describe how our perception of ourselves is influenced by others in our society, are the Attribution Theory and Social Comparison Theory. These will be explained in much greater detail in a later chapter of this book.

Undoubtedly, we let the perceptions of others affect ours as well. Sometimes, the effects can be good, and sometimes they are not so good. Regardless, we have an innate tendency to try and understand the behavior of others around us. This is our effort to try and become more acceptable members of society. We let the words and actions of others influence our views on situations and objects. Their memories influence their opinions and their perceptions, which then influence us.

Ultimately, the experiences we go through in life, from childhood to adulthood, become memories. These are both good and bad memories, and they stay with us for a very long time. Some stay with us forever. The emotions which are forged in our minds through these memories are also either good or bad. Like their associated memories, we carry these extremely powerful emotions with us for a lifetime.

Opinions are formed through these experiences and emotions, and opinions affect our perception of everything we see from then onwards. Thus, what we think is reality, is actually our perception of the world. In the next chapter, we will look at some powerful experiences, i.e. scenarios, which will help to further clarify how our experiences shape our perception of the world.

Chapter 1: 3 Mind-blowing Real Life Scenarios

In this chapter, we will present some real life examples which will attempt to clarify how our perception of reality is affected by our experiences in life.

Scenario 1 – Two Girls and a Dog

Consider two girls, Jane and Sarah. Both are quite young, maybe ten to fifteen years of age. They are good friends, and are taking a walk together in the park on a Sunday morning. They have both had their own experiences with dogs.

Sarah lives outside the city, and has been around dogs her entire life. Her father has kept dogs of numerous breeds around the house since before Sarah was born. Ever since she learned to crawl, walk and talk, her family dogs have been her companions. She is not afraid of them at all. She truly loves dogs, and considers them harmless animals that only want our love and attention.

Jane lives in the suburbs of the city, and had a neighbor who owned a Doberman Pinscher. One day, when playing outside on her own front porch, Jane casually strolled onto the curb of the road. While she was outside, her neighbor was walking his dog. He guided his dog in the direction in which Jane was playing, because he could not see her from far away.

As he and the dog came closer, Jane suddenly emerged onto the curb. The dog became alarmed, and immediately began pulling on the leash, and barking furiously. The neighbor could not restrain him, and let go of the leash. Jane was so frightened by the dog's barking and its fearsome appearance, that she screamed, and dashed for the door of her house. The dog chased her across her front porch, but she managed to outrun it. She locked the door to her house, and spent the entire day in her room, fearful and in tears.

Now we come back to the girls while they are walking in the park.

As they walk, hand in hand on the stone path, they see a woman with a Labrador Retriever on a leash approaching. Labrador Retrievers are very friendly and docile dogs, and they seldom behave aggressively towards humans. Upon seeing the dog, both girls exhibit very different reactions. Sarah, who has been with dogs her entire life, is happily surprised at seeing the Labrador. She becomes very excited and rushes towards the dog, in an attempt to cuddle the animal. Jane, however, behaves very differently.

Having had a rather traumatic experience with her neighbor's dog at a very early age, Jane is apprehensive, even afraid, of the approaching dog. She abandons her companion and retreats to a safe place close to a nearby tree, where she believes she will be safe.

The scenario described above is a classic example of how our past experiences influence our perceptions. Jane was frightened by a dog at a young age, and although the circumstances surrounding the event were unique in that the dog itself got alarmed at her sudden appearance, Jane's views on dogs remained firm. She continued to believe that they were harmful animals, and she feared them terribly.

When we look at Sarah, however, we see a loving affection towards dogs. Since she spent her early life in their company and never experienced an event similar to Jane's, she believes that dogs are friendly animals, and she is not at all afraid to pet them.

Now we will examine another scenario, which will help to explain the perception of a slightly more complex kind. Our general views on life, and the people around us, are influenced by our experiences as well. In the case of some people, these effects can be very strong, and can often completely warp their perception.

Scenario 2 – Same Place, But Different World

Consider Walter and James. Both are old men, in their eighties, and both live in the same old age home. They have become good acquaintances over the years, mainly because of the solitude which these homes provide. However, there is more to each of them than the observer can tell just by looking at their withered and fragile bodies.

James was born to a life of luxury. His father was an investment banker, and his mother was a dentist who owned a private clinic in a big city. James spent his childhood school days at a private boarding school, away from home. He was a very bright student, and as he grew, he developed an interest in the legal system. He decided to pursue a law degree at Columbia University, from where he received a scholarship.

During his time at Columbia, James excelled in his academics. On graduating, he obtained employment with a prestigious law firm. He made good money, and soon bought himself an apartment and a car. At the age of thirty, James married a woman he had fallen in love with. They lived together and she gave birth to a boy and a girl. Both children were as bright as their mother and father. The girl went on to study medicine, and the boy studied physics.

As James grew older and his children went to college, his mother passed away. He and his wife sold their apartment and moved into James' childhood home. His children married, and had children of their own. Eventually, James' wife passed away. His children, who all lived lives of their own, found a very decent and peaceful old age home, and decided to have him placed there. The house was sold, and James now lives in the old age home. His children and grandchildren come to visit him every week.

Now we consider Walter. Walter was born into a broken home. His father died before he was born, and he lost his mother at an early age as well. From then on, he was cared for by his uncle and aunt. He was not very good at school, trying desperately to skip classes, and always getting into trouble with other boys. As he became older, he decided to enlist in the military.

Walter fought in the Korean War; a war which had severe effects on those who participated in it and lived to tell their tales. Walter was one such person. As a soldier, he experienced the horrors of the war. He saw the bloodshed, he saw his comrades and best friends fall to the bullets of the enemies, and he carried their injured, and sometimes lifeless, bodies back to the barracks for treatment or burial.

After the war ended, Walter came back home a changed man and found a job as a truck driver. He married a few years later, and had three children. Although his children lived successful lives, Walter never moved out of an old house that he bought together with his wife. When she passed away, his children forced him to move to an old folks' home, so that they would not have to take care of him.

Now both men are in the old age home. But their attitudes are very different. James is a very pleasant person, who greets anyone who meets him, kindly. He is respectful towards the orderlies and the nurses, and he truly enjoys seeing his children when they visit.

Walter is different. He has been scarred by the harm which he has seen being committed in this world, and he has become indifferent towards other people, as an effect of the hostile attitude of his own children towards him. He absolutely does not enjoy the company of others and is very rude to the nurses and attendants.

In the above example, we saw how the experiences of a lifetime have an effect on our perception. James' views the world as a pleasant and wonderful place, while Walter resents everything about it.

In the final example, we will show how our environment and our culture have an effect on our perception.

Scenario 3 – Sun and Rain

The United Kingdom is notorious for being an extremely damp and rainy place. It would not be unfair to say that people there are generally sick of the weather, which remains cloudy and rainy for most of the year. Only during a very short spell in the summer months does the country experience a brief glow of the sun's warmth and shine. During that time, people enjoy sunbathing, outdoor activities, and chilled drinks. Soon after that, the autumn and winter seasons arrive, and are marked by cold showers and frosty snowfall.

On the other hand, consider a hot, dry and arid country-like Senegal or The Gambia. They recently experienced droughts, which brought about a massive famine. The general population starved, and the heat and dryness did not help make matters any better. Most people in the country would be unfamiliar with a UK-like winter.

Now consider someone from The Gambia traveling to the UK. He would probably be pleasantly surprised and very happy with the country's weather. He would thoroughly enjoy himself, and the rain, which he rarely sees in his own country, would be a refreshing boon to him. His native counterparts, on the other hand, would be quite fed-up with their own natural misfortune.

Thus, we have seen how our experiences shape our perception, and, therefore, how different people can have different views of the same situation. In the next chapter, we will take a look at some of the reasons for our varying perceptions of the world.

Chapter 2: Different Perceptions In The Same Experience

There are several factors which affect our perception. In the previous chapter, we looked at some general examples which showed how different people view the same event or scenario differently, based on their past experiences. In this chapter, we will examine the factors which affect our perception in more detail.

Past Experiences

We have already seen several examples of this. An early tumultuous encounter with a dog scarred a girl for life, while a childhood spent among the animals kindled a loving attitude towards them, in another. The psychological wounds of war are carried by people all their lives, while privilege and fortune can make a man see the world as a bright and shining place. Past experience is perhaps the most important factor which affects our perception of our reality. Its effects are the most visible, and most people carry opinions shaped by experience their entire lives.

Parents, Teachers and Friends

Our parents are the first people we see in this world. They are our guardians until we learn to take care of ourselves. It comes as no surprise then, that they have an immense effect on our perception. The way they treat us, care for us, and nurture us, all contribute to our understanding of the world, and our perception of reality. The same can be said for our teachers. They give us the knowledge which allows us to become confident, successful individuals. We see them as our role models, and they have a big influence on our perception. Our peers also contribute to our understanding of the world. Their presence gives us hope and courage.

Religion

Our religion is a major part of our upbringing. It directly affects who we are as people. It influences our morality, our judgment and our view of the world. It teaches us compassion, justice and equality, and it allows us to focus on goals which are of a different category than our worldly desires. Depending on which part of the world you are from, and your ancestral lineage, your religion could be very conservative or quite liberal. Of course, this affects the way we learn to live our lives, the way we view other people and how much value we attach to material desires.

Financial State

This is another very important factor which influences our perception. We saw in the second example in the previous chapter, how a difference in financial upbringing creates differences in the way that people see the world and others around themselves. People, who grow up in wealthy families and receive adequate education usually, view the world as being full of opportunities. They want to explore it and become wealthy and successful. Others from less privileged backgrounds generally view the world as a cruel and inconsiderate place. Even though they also sometimes become successful, it is through a different set of desires altogether.

Type of Residence

This is, of course, directly tied to the previous factor, i.e. financial state. Our lives are centered on our home from the moment we take our first breath. It becomes a place of peace, comfort, relaxation and solace. Our home is a very dear place to all of us and the kind of home we live in has an effect on our perception of the world. The vastly wealthy, with their immense estates, have a different view of the world from someone who lives in an apartment, or a trailer. Similarly, some people do not even have a home and live on the streets. This obviously changes their perception of the world.

Family Background

We have already established how important the effects of your parents are on your perception of the world. Generally, your entire family and upbringing have an equally important effect. The sort of lifestyle you lived as a child, or even as an adolescent, influences your attitude towards life and what you believe the world is like. If you come from a broken home, i.e. if you have divorced parents, or one of your parents is deceased, then that will strongly affect your outlook on life.

Abuse is often linked to the development of psychological abnormalities in children who suffer from it and can lead to a bleak view of the world. Some children grow up in homes where parents might be addicted to drugs or alcohol. In these cases, it is quite likely that the children will learn to take care of themselves. They may begin to see the world as an uncaring and unwelcoming place, where one must struggle to survive. Children who grow up watching their parents do drugs might begin doing the same at some stage in their lives.

The importance of home has already been discussed, but the area of town where you live is also very important. The type of people vary greatly, depending on what part of town you live in, and you may be influenced by their standard of living, as well as your own living arrangements. Early exposure to crime, prostitution, drugs and other illegal activities can have severely detrimental effects on a child in some cases. Children learn to think of these activities as the only way to make a living and when they grow older, they may become involved in them.

Media

The media has an extremely powerful influence on our perception of the world. Not always, but quite often, the truth is stretched and altered slightly by the digital and print media, before it is presented to the people. This obviously affects what people see and what they believe is the truth behind the events occurring around the world or in their own community.

Someone living in a first world country would hear a news broadcast that a roadside bomb in some country in the Middle East has killed twenty people and start believing that the entire Middle East in an unsafe place. Tabloids continue to report celebrity headlines on front page articles and people begin associating themselves with these celebrities and their jet-setting lifestyles.

Chapter 3: Getting Inside A Thought

In this chapter, we will attempt to explore the process of forming a perception and how it relates directly to the way you think, i.e. to your stream of thought. By understanding the thought process, you can start to improve the way you think, change your perception and thus, change your outlook on life.

We have already established how your reality is, in fact, your perception of the world and others around you. This is a very important conclusion, since a positive or negative perception can affect your outlook on life. People with positive perceptions tend to see the world as a place full of opportunities, hope and happiness, albeit with its fair share of struggles and worries. These people generally tend to see things through a kaleidoscope-like lens. They see the beauty in the world around them and they are quite optimistic about their life and experiencing new things. A positive perception encourages a healthy and happy lifestyle.

On the other hand, people with negative perceptions are very critical about the world and the people in their lives. They see the world as a cruel and unforgiving place, where the struggle to survive is marred by the unkindness of the people around them and the distressing events in their lives leave scars which are carried around for a lifetime.

We have already seen, in the second scenario presented in the first chapter, how different the perception of Walter was from that of James. Again, the root cause of this difference in perception lies in the events and experiences which one goes through in early life. It may also be rooted in one's genetics, upbringing and social/financial state. Generally, however, a negative perception rises out of a combination of several of the above-mentioned factors, having an unhealthy effect on the mind of a person.

A negative perception can have severe effects on a person's state of mind, particularly if the person's outlook presents to him a world which is bleak and malevolent. A resigned and pessimistic attitude towards the world can be very distressing for an individual. If your perception is not helping you achieve happiness and success in life, then you need to change it. The first and most important step, in changing your outlook is the realization that you need to do so.

Without realizing the need to change their perception, a person cannot begin to make changes for his betterment. However, since the cause of a negative perception is deeply rooted in a person's experiences, genetics, finances and all these have a cumulative effect, it can be very hard to realize that you need to change. Individuals who have developed set skills of perception find it very difficult to change their views on objects, people and events, particularly if they are in their middle age. A mind-set used to observing scenarios from a particular point of view will not be able to vary that point of view after years and years of experiences.

However, the strength to change lies in your heart and your willpower. If you firmly believe that you need to change, then believing that you can alter your perception is really half the battle already won. Once you start believing, you can start to understand your own thoughts. You need to understand your thought process, the way your mind works and the way you reach conclusions, in order to change your perception.

Once you learn to observe your own thoughts, you will start to see patterns emerging. You should pay particular attention to how you reach important decisions, which affect your life. This is quite difficult for most people, but again, it all depends on your personal strength. A good way to understand and observe your thoughts is to imagine a scenario that has a certain moral, personal and social importance to you. Imagine conversations you would have with people regarding the subject, and record your immediate thoughts and responses.

Once you start to understand your stream of thought, you will start to see how you reach decisions. Try and understand the factors which you consider when making decisions. You will almost definitely consider your chances of success by making the decision and how it will help you achieve that success. You will also consider how your personal confidence will be affected by the decision, as well as your social standing and image.

You can then begin to understand the root causes behind your decision. Could they arise out of childhood experiences? Are they the effects of your education, or your parents or teachers? You will then learn to understand why you perceive things the way that you do.

An awareness of your perception is one of the most important steps in improving your outlook on life. As we have seen in the introduction section, the process of perception is very complex. It may take a lot of time and effort before you begin to understand how your mind works, and notice patterns in your stream of thought. Some people consult therapists and psychologists, in order to explore the depths of their mind and learn more about themselves.

Finally, another very important part of improving your perception, and to make better decisions, is to observe successful people, who are happy with their lives and make good decisions. Pay attention to their attitudes, their demeanor and their mannerism. You can learn a lot from them, particularly from the way that they make decisions. Read the biographies of some of the most successful people in the world. Billionaires, philanthropists, scientists, inventors and revolutionaries all have led very interesting lives, and you can learn a lot from their experiences.

Through a proper understanding of your thought process, your decision making abilities, and the causes deep-seated causes behind your actions, you can learn to change your perception. Only through an understanding of your perception, can you change your outlook on life.

Chapter 4: The Perception Transformation

Your perception is the way you see the world. As we have discussed in the previous chapter, a negative perception can have pernicious effects on your life, and a positive perception can be a liberating and beneficial thing. Therefore, changing your perception could be the best thing you do in your life. In this chapter, we will attempt to explain changing one's perception and the motivation behind bringing about this change. We will look at techniques and methods that can help you achieve this, so you can adopt a positive and healthy attitude towards life.

There are several reasons why you would want to change your perception. However, the most obvious and overwhelming factor is that a negative perception makes you very unhappy. It forces you to live an unhealthy and unproductive lifestyle, and hinders you from living life to the fullest or achieving the success that you deserve. Sometimes, you may not have what one would call a negative perception, but you may want to change the way you think and make decisions, if your current perception is not helping you accomplish your goals.

Regardless of what you feel you need to change your perception is, there are ways that you can begin to understand the process of forming one and then alter it. This has been described in the previous chapter; it mainly involves an understanding of the thought process and how you eventually reach conclusions or form opinions.

You may be unhappy with yourself in your present lifestyle and the outcomes of your decisions. You may not be achieving financial success, personal satisfaction, social appeal, mental peace of mind or a generally healthy and prosperous lifestyle. However, you may also feel that certain factors beyond your control, which are mostly generalized as the pressures created by a vibrant social atmosphere, are causing your unhappiness. In this case, realizing that your perception is the root cause behind your disappointments can be very difficult. People seldom believe, or rather want to believe, that there is something wrong with them, instead of the world around them.

The bottom line here, is that your perception could be making you very unhappy in life, and therefore you should definitely change it.

When we looked at the causes behind the development of one's perception of events and objects, we saw how it was deeply rooted in that person's experiences. These experiences could be based in one's childhood, adolescence or even their adulthood.

Failures tend to affect a person's outlook and thought process the most severely, and we carry our failures with us for a long time. Although it is good to do that, because we learn a lot from our failures, dwelling too much on them can warp our perception in an unhealthy way.

Equally detrimental can be the effects of dwelling on one's successes for too long, as well. This may also change one's perception in an unhealthy way. Finding the right balance, and allowing certain events to affect you and others do not, is very difficult for most people. Furthermore, as a person approaches adulthood, changing one's mental attitude is a very complex and stressing endeavor, but one which eventually comes down to the person's strength of character and will.

Thus, we see that many things can affect our perception and therefore, changing one's perception can be very difficult. Our minds are attuned to viewing certain events, objects and individuals as positive and others as negative. Thus to change one's perception would require to open one's mind and allow it to form completely new opinions which are unaffected by previous experiences and events.

When we spoke about observing others people's behavior and their decisions in the previous chapter, the idea being conveyed was that you allow yourself to understand how and why they consider certain scenarios as positive and others as negative. If the majority consider a certain event as positive and you think of it as negative, ask yourself why.

Sometimes, you may need to force yourself to think of something as positive, even when your gut instinct goes completely against this. You will eventually begin to see the bright side of things, even those which are negative. This is the beginning of a change. Once you start to see how even the most devastating failures have a bright side, you will know that your perception has taken a turn for the better. As you go on in life and continue with your positive thought provoking practices, recording your thoughts and learning to transform your negative perception into a positive one will become much easier and you will notice a change.

When dealing with failure, you must realize that although a failure in any aspect of your life will invariably cause scars, you must learn to rise above failure. You must rise above the anchoring effect that failure has on your drive and start seeing how your failure will help you become a better person. Any failure, or any bad experience for that matter, teach you a lot. The important thing is not to let a single bad experience severely affect your perception.

Perhaps the simplest example, which demonstrates the veracity of this claim, is when you go out to eat at a restaurant that you have never eaten at before. You do not know what the food is like, so you go there to experiment. When the food arrives, you find that it is well below your expectations and in fact, when you go home you get mild food poisoning.

So you decide never to eat again at that same restaurant. What you should not do is to stop eating at restaurants altogether, just because you had one bad experience. Keep your mind open, allow yourself to experience new things and learn to see the positive side of bad things. You will now know that that particular restaurant serves bad food, so you will never eat there again.

If you can learn to change your perception, you can focus on exactly what you want to see in a certain scenario. You should also avoid 'filter thinking', which means hearing only what you want to hear when something is communicated to you. Another very common mental compulsion is what is colloquially known as 'catastrophizing'. This means that you should avoid thinking that everything is going to end in a distressing conclusion. This is very devastating and can cause you to resign from making any effort before you even begin.

You need to focus on positive things. First of all, you need to ask yourself what is it that you want to see. The answer to this would generally be that you want to see how even the bad elements of a scenario are beneficial to you, so that you can learn to be positive about them. But that is easier said than done. So how do you focus on the positive side of things which your perception would normally make you think of as negative?

The simple uplifting truth behind any failure, or any bad experience, is that it will help you become stronger. It will enable you to make better decisions and become a better person, but only if you allow it to do so. If you let your failures change your perception, so that you resign from your endeavors and lose your drive for achieving success altogether, then you will be very unhappy with your life. Getting back up after a failure is one of the hardest things you will ever have to do in life, but if you manage to do it, you will feel better, stronger and move closer to achieving success. The words of Maya Angelou capture this best of all.

"You may encounter many defeats, but you must not be defeated. In fact, it may be necessary to encounter the defeats, so you can know who you are, what you can rise from, how you can still come out of it."

History presents us with its own examples of people who failed at first, but then they rose above their failures, and achieved true greatness. J.K. Rowling, the renowned author of the Harry Potter novel series, was rejected by numerous publishing houses before her books were finally published. She was also divorced, unemployed and raising her daughter on her own.

Henry Ford, the great automobile magnate, watched as the early business of his company forced it into severe bankruptcy. Today he is considered one of the greatest entrepreneurs of all time. Winston Churchill was a terrible student in his early days, failing the sixth grade. As a politician, he was defeated in every public office role which he contested, but later went on to become the British Prime Minister. Albert Einstein was considered a slow student by his teachers and professors. However, his contributions to the field of Physics won him the Nobel Prize in 1921.

Had any of the above-mentioned people thrown in the towel when they first failed, the world would have been a very different place, for the worse. Thankfully, they did not. They looked beyond their disappointments by continuing to struggle and think positively. The fruits of their efforts are evident from the way their achievements changed the very fabric of human thinking.

You must try your best to avoid what is known as 'black and white' thinking. In this type of thinking you only consider things as either good or bad, i.e. there are no shades of grey. In order to open yourself up to new opinions and experiences, so you can see the bright side of things, you must embrace these shades of grey. They will keep your mind from generalizing or reaching quick and rash decisions.

Another aspect of changing your perception, is taking responsibility for your actions. After all, your thoughts are your own and nobody else's. This again, is very hard for a lot of people to accept, but it is a truth that you need to deal with. This does not mean that you should think that if anything goes wrong, it is automatically your fault. There are a lot of things that go wrong in our everyday lives, and if you start blaming yourself for every such event, you will make yourself even more miserable and paranoid.

Positive thinking will be directly advantageous to your lifestyle. You will take control of your life and your mental and physical health will improve. Aside from that, positive thinking has been shown to be linked to an increased lifespan and lower depression. Believe it or not, a positive outlook on life has also been shown to improve your resistance to diseases such as the common cold! A positive perception allows you to deal effectively with stress, and become more pleasant towards your relatives and friends.

We have already discussed how you can understand your thought process. You do this by recording your thoughts. This can be very therapeutic if you are trying to think positively. Keep a diary in which you record your feelings and can reflect upon them later. By doing this, you can see exactly how negative thoughts and perceptions arise in your sub-conscience, and then you can gradually begin to eliminate them from your stream of thought. You can do the same with stress. Notice events and thoughts which cause your stress levels to rise.

Conclusion

In this book, we have looked at how we form perceptions and how we can start to alter our perception if we are unhappy with ourselves. The process of forming a perception is very complex and our perceptions are built into the very fabric of our personality. They take form when we are very young and evolve as we grow older.

Your willingness and strength of character are perhaps your biggest tools for attempting to change your perception. This change will not be easy and you may feel like quitting at some stage. The seeds planted in us during our childhood and early adulthood are very difficult to uproot, and you will find it difficult to change your long-held opinions and perception. However, as we have stressed in the previous chapter, it all depends on how much you want to adopt a happy and healthy lifestyle.

Learn to study your thoughts. Understand your thought process and try to reach the root cause of your unhappiness. Then open yourself to new ideas, by scrapping old ones. Focus on the things which you really need from life, the good things, and the things which will help you achieve success.

As with any new endeavor, which is meant to bring about a drastic change to one's lifestyle, changing your perception takes time. You will undoubtedly become impatient when you try to change your view of the world, events, people and general ideas. Adopting a positive attitude and perception is a skill which takes time and dedication to develop. Again, this is linked to your upbringing.

Do not let your negative perception affect you through your failures. Instead, you must learn to accept your failures and rise above them. Keep yourself engaged and positive by saying positive, constructive things to yourself. This will keep you emotionally pleasant and encouraged. You will be happy with yourself and your accomplishments. Praise yourself for the things you do well and do not dwell on those you are not accomplished at.

Be open to new experiences. This is perhaps one of the most important lessons you should take away from this book. Keeping an open mind is a large part of opening up to new opinions and a whole new perception. You have a long and prosperous life ahead of you, and if you begin to negate new people, places, objects, and events by having a narrow worldview, then you will never be able to enjoy the beauty and wonder of things.

Avoid generalizations and learn to appreciate new things. Eat at a new restaurant, go and visit a new city (or maybe even a new country), take acting or dance classes in order to relax, read new books, learn to play a musical instrument and learn a new language. All these will open you up to new experiences and hence, new ways of looking at the world.

Be aware of your thoughts. Once you have understood your stream of thought and your pattern for reaching the decisions that provoke a negative perception, you can avoid detrimental thoughts. Sometimes, a negative perception is formed when one tries to create a shield around oneself against bad experiences and feelings. Try and open yourself up, and always be aware of your how you perceive things around you.

Meditation is a very powerful and effective technique. People all around the world use it to achieve mental peace and reduce their stress levels. Try taking up meditation, if you have the time. Even if you do not, try making time in your day for a quiet and relaxing meditation session. It only takes 10 to 20 minutes, and you will feel amazingly relaxed. Do it in a quiet place, where there are no distractions and no one can disturb you.

As a form of meditation, start reading books. This can be very therapeutic and it will undoubtedly give you mental peace. Read biographies of the great people or classics in fiction. When you set aside a certain time of the day just for reading, you will see that it will allow you to reflect on your own thoughts, while simultaneously encouraging creative contemplation. Books will stimulate your imagination and give you precious peace of mind. Travel books will open you up to new cultures, adventure books will encourage your creativity and the classics will allow you to explore your ideas and opinions on critical topics. Reading may also spark your creativity and encourage you to start writing!

Do something creative. Perhaps there is something that you have always wanted to do, but you never gave much thought to it because you thought you were too busy. Now is the time to start doing it! Maybe you are interested in photography. Get yourself a camera and let your imagination run wild. Or, maybe you want to learn sketching; is so, then take up amateur art classes. The point is that you should allow yourself to exercise your imagination and creativity. This will be a liberating experience.

Spend time with people who are successful and who take on the world confidently. Learn from them and their attitude to understand their perception. Get to know them and allow their failures to teach you as well. Try and find out how these people keep themselves motivated, and then adopt an attitude that will allow you to be as motivated and successful as them. Avoid taking antidepressants or any other sort of medication without first consulting a psychiatrist. They are very harmful to help if taken in the wrong dosage or without proper instruction.

By adopting the changes and attitudes described in this book, you will definitely change your perception about life, people and events. This change might be subtle at first, but the key is not to give up. Adopting a positive attitude, opening yourself to new experiences and seeing the bright side of things will be very beneficial to you. Allowing yourself to develop a positive perception is a crucial step on the way to achieving happiness in life.

Lateral Thinking

How To Apply Lateral Thinking To Everyday Life

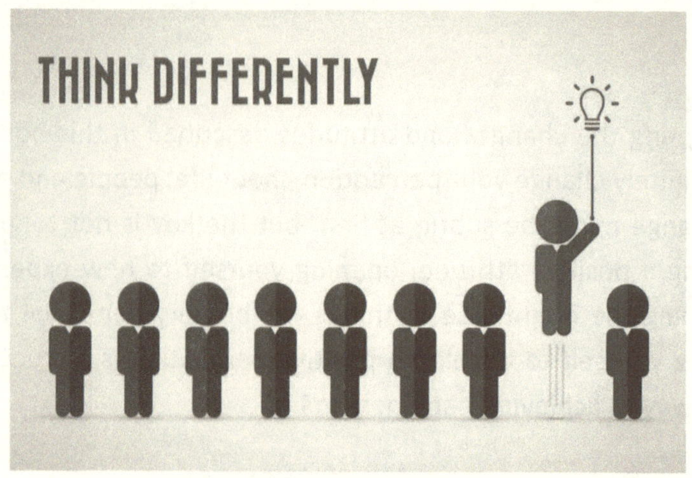

A GUIDE ON EXPANDING YOUR CREATIVE HORIZONS

Chris Smythe

Contents

listen to your heart.
Live in harmony, fully understand, accept and embrace who you are.
Listening to your heart

Conclusion

Introduction

Living in a modern society is not easy. Maybe we sometimes look back at the people that lived way before us in the age where no technology existed and we tend to feel sorry for them because we think it was much harder living back then, but trust me, they had one thing that is much more valuable than technology or anything else that we have in the modern age. It is the peace of mind. And what does peace of mind help us with? The most important thing that humans were created to do. Thinking correctly, freely and **without the influence of others**. Unlike people today, they didn't have any worry about what others thought about them and they certainly did not do things against their will just so they can feel like they fit in. They lived their lives freely and the way they wanted. The only way life is meant to be lived.

Before I begin, I want you to read and give a completely honest answer to all of my following questions.

Do you maybe sometimes feel like you're doing something against your will or making a certain decision without really being sure why exactly you're doing it? Do you often look at what others are doing and decide that you should be doing those exact same things, just so that you can be accepted in the community and feel like a part of it? Do you feel like a black sheep in the herd if you're the only one that's doing something differently from all your friends or family? Are you afraid of making changes? Do you often spend time on social media or in front of a TV screen watching reality shows or following celebrities? Is the fear of failure dragging you down and pushing you far away from reaching your goals and making your dreams come true?

If the answer is "YES" to any of these questions, then I really think you might want to reconsider the way you think, your decision-making abilities and honestly ask yourself if you are living the way you truly want or simply living to please the others around you.

In this book, I will personally share my own experiences, interesting situations and thoughts with you, and help you clear your mind of all the anxiety and worry and constantly remind you that you don't have to care about being like the others around you or think a certain way just because others are doing it.

It is time to start using your mind the way it should be used, make the decisions that are right and beneficial for you and remember who you really were before society or social media told you who you are.

I will give my best to make you realize some of the very important details, aspects and secrets of life that you might have missed while you were stuck in the endless loop of modern life and help you learn how to start thinking on your own and do what is best for you. I will be talking about the <u>Lateral Thinking</u> method also known as "Thinking outside of the Box", explaining how it works and why it is very beneficial for us to learn it and utilize it in our everyday life. I will also cover many different topics on how we think, why sometimes our decisions are very influenced by the others, how most of the people are forced to think a certain way since their young age, how to admit that you've made a mistake and utilize it as a lesson in life, why changes are a very necessary thing in life, how other people easily get tricked into changing their beliefs and much more.

 I am going to teach you all of the useful elements which I applied when I was learning how to **"Think outside of the Box"**. I will talk to you about the traditional "vertical thinking" method and its flaws and ultimately transfer all of my valuable knowledge and experience to you. Remember, if you don't want to change yourself, nobody else can. Change starts from within, and if you learn the importance of it, learn how to utilize Lateral Thinking and overall understand the way our brain works, you will be able to master the way you think and live a much happier and fulfilling life.

Without further ado, let's dive deep into our first chapter. It will be a long and wonderful journey full of interesting stories and experiences that happened in my past, as well as many situations that require good decision-making abilities in which you might find yourself in at any moment of your life.

Chapter 1: What is Lateral Thinking aka "Thinking outside of the box?"

The purpose of why we think is to be able to collect information and attempt to make the best possible use out of it. Because of how our mind works and creates patterns, we are not able to make the best use out of the new information unless we find a way to reconstruct the old patterns and bring them up to date. Not everyone can do this because from our very young age we are trained to use the traditional thinking method. The "traditional" method that we use or also known as "vertical thinking" only teaches us how to select some of the already existing patterns and make a decision through a process of elimination. However, we will never get the best out of our decisions if we don't learn how to utilize the Lateral Thinking method.

Lateral thinking or "Thinking outside of the box" is a term used to describe a method of solving problems or making decisions by using a more indirect or "unusual" and creative approach, most often by looking at the "problem" from a different perspective. People who are such thinkers are not worried about the opinions of others and always tend to make decisions that are good for them, regardless if someone else thinks otherwise. Lateral thinking is very tightly related to creativity, humor, and insight. By utilizing all of these things our mind is able to re-wire and make a superior decision and get the best out of every situation that we find ourselves in.

Here are a few examples to help you understand better. Many people often start to do what their family or friends do, just so that they can feel like a part of the group. For example, I personally know many people who really and I mean really dislike smoking cigarettes but they started doing it because everyone else in their friend circle was smoking, or because the girl that they liked smoked as well and they just wanted to fit in or impress them. They are going against their will and in this case against their health just so they feel more comfortable. Another example is when a friend calls you and says that he watched a movie and that movie was awful, so If you watch it, you will constantly see everything in a bad light and nothing will impress you. This is because your friend's opinion matters a lot to you and can often blur out your real perception of things. Same would be if you were to buy a pair of jeans and your friend tells you that they look very good on your body even though they don't. You will still convince yourself that they do match you, just because he said so.

Here is a short story from when I was in high school.
I went out to a party with a friend from my class. Before going there, we both agreed that we will just stay sober, socialize with others and have a good "chill" time without drinking much or do anything crazy. At some point in the night, a group of guys from our class came and we clearly saw that they are under the effect of psychedelic drugs. I suggested to my friend that we leave and go somewhere else to avoid a problem. Sadly, we were not really quick in our decision making and they got real close to us. We got into a small talk and they started making fun of my friend because he wasn't drinking or doing any drugs, and knowing his personality, he got really upset and worried that they will keep teasing him about it if he doesn't prove them wrong. His ego was very fragile and without much hesitation, he asked them to give him whatever they took and he will prove to them that he is not what they think he is. After a few attempts to stop him, I finally gave up because all he cared about is the reputation "he would get" if he just stopped being a coward. I made a final attempt at convincing him that this is a very bad decision, but he just swallowed the pills. After half an hour, he is laying on a hospital bed, his father is talking to the police, his mom can't stop crying and my parents are freaking out and yelling at me saying that I was supposed to be the one to stop him from doing that. After a two week period when everything settles down, he comes back to school and guesses what happens. Not only that they didn't

stop calling him a coward, but they also made fun of him even more now for being "weak" and getting sick from just a couple of pills.

The point of my story is that by making one bad decision just so that he can be what someone else wants him to be, he created even more problems for himself. He worsened his health and now he is being teased and called out even more. Not to mention all of the punishments from his parents and the bad picture that he left in everyone's eyes.

If he would just reject doing drugs, everyone would look at him like a smart guy who can stand up for himself and make smart decisions. Maybe he would even convince those guys who teased him that drugs are bad for their health. He is a smart guy, but his worry about being accepted in a certain group and the need to prove himself all the time to someone is what really ruined him. In this example my friend was thinking using the traditional "vertical thinking" method, he excluded one out of two situations and picked the one he thought will be the best which later reflected really bad on him. Instead, if he used the lateral thinking method he would be able to create new pathways and create a situation that is to his advantage. He could've politely reject doing drugs, start a talk about how drugs are bad and unhealthy and how they should stop using them as well. This would make the group of guys look at him in completely different light and instead of calling him a coward they will form an image in their heads that he is, in fact, a smart guy and he worries about their good being. He could've been the hero of the night instead of ending up in the hospital bed, and he could've made some new friends as well. This way he ended up getting the worst case scenario because in his mind there were only two options, he did not see the countless other ones because he was thinking vertically.

My example might have been a little harsh, but it's the sad truth and this happens almost all the time in our everyday lives. We need to constantly ask ourselves why we're doing something and is it the right thing to do. Let "is this truly what I want" be the phrase you always hear in your mind before doing something. Taking drugs was not what he wanted at all, he wanted to be appreciated and accepted and he thought that there is only one way to do it.

Chapter 2: Why we do what we do.

In the introduction part, I mentioned a term called "following the herd".

This is often used to describe someone who blindly follows a group (or so-called a "herd") without questioning their decisions or thinking for themselves. Sometimes the "sheep" is a person who was just raised and "taught" to follow what others are doing without questioning in order to avoid risks or other sorts of challenges. Even if it may sound a bit weird at first, people like this really exist. They just want to be in their comfort zones so much that it doesn't even matter to them that they're completely the same as somebody else. They don't know the powers, qualities and unique capabilities that they possess, and usually, when someone tries to talk to them about it, they would get angry. Others are heavily influenced by social media and they tend to look at celebrities or some of the idols that they have and try to live, look or act exactly like them.

They try to wear the same types of clothes, dye their hair the same color, try to talk with their accent, get the same tattoos and maybe even change their religion like them. They change their image completely just so they can look or feel like them.

I will begin this chapter with another example, also a real story that happened to me in my teen years as well.

I was out with a group of friends in a park just having a good time and listening to some music. Suddenly a discussion about religion pops out and everyone engages in it. After some time a guy that sits right next to me is asked the next question: Are you religious and do you believe in God?
His answer was the following:

I am very religious, I go to church every week and I pray on the table with my family before eating dinner, but I do not believe in God.

Everyone just stopped talking for a minute and gave him a very confused look. A girl then asks him: Why would you do all of those things if you simply don't believe in God?

He says: **I do all of those things because everyone in my family is doing it.** They are very religious and if they find out that I'm not, they will never look at me the same way and probably see me as a heretic and I will feel like an outcast. I'm afraid to tell them that I just don't believe, so I just keep pretending that I do and keep getting involved in their religious activities.

This is the moment when I realized that some people are just doing things because they're afraid to be different and honest with themselves. I understand that in the dark ages being a non-believer was a problem, I really do, but I honestly think that in modern times people should not feel like black sheep just because they don't want to follow a certain religion or some kind of a movement.

The sad truth is that people tend to do what others do, they like a certain type of music just because their friends like the same, not realizing that the ones who stand out and are unique, are usually the most attractive and smart people in everyone's eyes.

If you don't like a certain song, tell your friends why. Give out your opinion on it. If someone asks you if their shirt looks good on them when it really doesn't, give them the harsh truth. Don't say things that are not true and against your will hoping that someone will like you more because of it. You're just doing them a favor by telling them the truth. You will actually be surprised by how many people will appreciate your honest thoughts and most likely thank you for them. In a society where everyone lies to impress others, be a beacon of honesty and pure thoughts, it's the most attractive thing ever. And if someone gets mad at and starts insulting you for telling the truth, it means you only did yourself a favor, they just let you know that they were never a good person and you don't need those kinds of people in your life.

People need to get out of their comfort zones, they need to have their own strong opinions about the things that they like or dislike. They need to stand up and fight for what they love even if it means losing a "friend" or leaving a bad impression on someone. Stop looking and taking examples from famous people on social media or reality shows. If they buy expensive cars, clothes and god knows what else, it does not mean that you have to be exactly like them. We are constantly being manipulated and have fake images created in our mind about how we are supposed to look, dress, eat or talk. Stop worrying about not having enough money to buy expensive clothes whatever reason you need them for, beauty comes from within.

Stop worrying and stressing about what others think, it's your own life and you need to live it the way you want, not the way others want.

Social conditioning is a term used to describe a process when individuals are being trained in a society to have certain beliefs, emotional reactions, desires and wishes, behaviors and things of that nature, which are approved by that same society in general or by some groups that are part of it.

This social conditioning process usually begins from your very early age and it is most effective or "acute" during your childhood and adolescence, but it can keep going through your entire life. This is almost always carried by teachers, people in your community, parents, the TV shows that you watch, the novels that you read, the church that you go to every Sunday, the ads that you see and media as a whole and many other factors.

It does not really matter if you are aware of it or not, but we are being conditioned to act and do things in a certain way just because others around us are doing it.

The sad thing is that social conditioning usually works in a way by repeating and putting things in our brain millions and millions of times until our consciousness finally gives up and absorbs all of the unhealthy information. For example, every time you turn on a TV you see a guy that is dressed in expensive brands and has big muscles and the girls "drool" over him, which slowly puts an image in your mind that if you dress expensively or if you get big muscles girls will automatically "drool" over you as well.

Ever since we were kids our parents taught us to socialize with others and do activities together. Even if this sounds like a good thing, in some cases it can really be bad when it comes to our decision making. We learn to constantly look at others and what they're doing and if we do something different we start feeling guilt and worry that we're not "normal". Ask yourself an honest question.

What does really "being normal" mean to you? What does even "normal" mean to you as a term? I'll give you ten seconds to answer.

Is your answer similar to this?

"Being normal means doing what everyone else is doing. "

If it is, then we have a problem.

It's time for a life story again..
There is a 16-year-old boy called James that really enjoys playing video games. He spends most of his time after school playing online. His parents realize that simply their kid loves what he's doing and don't force him to stop doing it. He has some friends from school, not all of them like playing video games, but he has one that really does. That friend's name is Rick. They both play games together and are very passionate about it, but unlike James's parents, Rick's parents constantly yell at him for doing it. They think video games are going to ruin him and that playing them is not "normal" at all. Instead, he must do things that are "normal". Rick is being forced to go outside when he doesn't want and forced to play football which he really hates. This impacts Rick's emotions because he's torn away from doing what he loves, this translates to him losing attention in class because he constantly thinks about video games, then he starts getting bad grades and gets punished at home. His parents still think that they're doing a good job. Meanwhile, James is happy because his parents let him do what he loves, he has really good grades and he is slowly becoming very good at the game he plays. A few years go by and now James is a professional gamer with a good salary, he is given a scholarship to many different high-grade universities and becomes pretty famous among others. He starts meeting new friends because of it and he is living his dream. Rick on the opposite is now left with nothing. He is not good at football because he hates doing it, he doesn't have a scholarship because his grades are bad and he's very sad because his parents restricted him from making his dreams come true. This is a prime example of how forcing someone to do something that is considered "normal" can only have a very bad impact on the person.

The point of this story is that people sometimes are forced since their young age to do something they hate just because someone else thinks it is right and "normal".

Nobody should be forced to be "normal" and do what others do. Everyone should get a chance to make their dreams come true. If you are brave, believe in your goals and constantly get out of your comfort zone, you will always reach your goals.

You should not upgrade your phone every year because everyone else is doing it. You should not feel pressure to get married and have a family at an age that you don't want that to happen, just because everyone else is doing it. There are no rules in this world about how to live your life. Be yourself and do what you love. Everything else will come right to its place, stop forcing things.

Staring at a computer screen or a TV will not bring you any clarity or wisdom. You need to stop wasting time watching reality shows or looking at Instagram pages and other social media. The harsh truth is that it is indeed brainwashing you and altering your mind, making you think incorrectly. Each time you open up Instagram and you take a look at how the celebrities and the rich people live, and you create false expectations in your mind about how you should live, and if you don't get that kind of a life, you are disappointed by yourself and you think that you are miserable. You keep looking at models that wear expensive pieces of clothes that cost over ten thousands of dollars and you think that you are poor and unhappy, when in fact you really aren't. Remember that there are people in this world without a roof over their heads and without a clean water to drink that usually die from infections and other diseases, do you really think that they care about Instagram followers or expensive brands and designer clothes? I don't think so no. Most of the people are even addicted to such reality shows but they are not even aware of it. Kids nowadays tend to freak out if the internet connection or electricity goes out for a few minutes. It makes me feel like everyone is so addicted to living in the fake virtual social media worlds that it becomes utterly disgusting. I don't want to start that cliché talk about how we used to play hide and seek but kids nowadays don't because they are stuck in front of their computer screens, but when you really think about it, that "talk" slowly starts to become the sad reality. My honest opinion is that you should focus on doing things that will later help you ensure an existence for you, your family and your loved ones. If you really want to have a career in playing video games then yes, give your best and I hope you will make it, but if you spend your time on the internet watching celebrities and how they live while creating fake images of how you should live your life, then you are really harming yourself.

Chapter 4: "Thinking outside of the box"

Most people don't think outside of the box, not because they can't but because they are afraid of being judged or being called "weird". Just like the example which I mentioned before about the guy who followed religion and religious traditions just because his family was doing it.
The truth is that we are all weird in a different way. Each of us is unique and we need to understand and embrace that. The sooner we realize this, the better for us.

Lateral thinking arises from the way our mind works. Our information handling system that is called "mind" is highly effective but it has its own limitations. Those limitations are inseparable from the advantages of the system because both are coming directly from the nature of the system. It is impossible to get the advantages without the disadvantages. Lateral thinking is meant to compensate for the disadvantages while you can still enjoy the advantages.

Most people believe that the traditional so-called "vertical thinking" is the only possible and effective way of thinking. We need to look at the lateral thinking and understand how it works so that we can recognize the advantages compared to the vertical thinking method.

Vertical thinking is all about **rightness**, lateral thinking is all about **richness**. Vertical thinking often selects one path and excludes all of the other pathways. Lateral thinking works very differently. Instead of excluding paths it creates new paths that are otherwise invisible with vertical thinking.

With vertical thinking, a person will select the most promising approach when attempting to solve a problem. With lateral thinking, the person will try to generate as many different and alternative approaches possible. **If there's no way, you need to make one.** Vertical thinking takes you on a pathway only if one exists, lateral thinking helps you create a pathway. A lot of pathways.

With vertical thinking, a person will use the "negative" in a situation to be able to block and eliminate certain paths. With lateral thinking, there will be no "negative" in a situation. Lateral thinking is all about the "Glass half full, not half empty" approach.

One of the most perfect examples of lateral thinking and creating pathways or "Thinking outside the box" that I've ever heard is this one:

A guy is asked the following:
You are driving in your car on a very rainy day on your way home, and you get close to a bus stop. You slow down a bit and look at the people waiting in the rain with no ride. You look closely and realize that one of them is your best friend who once saved your life, the other one is the perfect woman of your dreams and the third one is a lonely old lady that looks really sick.
You can only take one person in your car and take them home. Which person would you choose? The people who asked him this thought that they tricked them because no matter what he chose he had to give up on something that is important to him. Do you pick up the old lady because she is in a very bad condition, or do you pick your best friend because he once saved your life? Either way, you are losing the woman of your dreams that you always loved.

The answer that he gave stunned everyone in the room. This is what he said:
I would give the keys of my car to my friend, he can drive the old lady back home and then get home safely himself, he will return the car later or tomorrow, and I will stay with the woman of my dreams and wait for the bus together.

This guy literally got the best possible outcome from the given situation. A prime example of lateral thinking and very good decision making abilities. He did not exclude all of his options in order to get only one and use that one. He instead made many new pathways and solved many problems at once, unlike the vertical thinking method which would've solved only one problem.

Now a vertical thinker would start excluding options, in this case, people, and find what option will benefit him the most. Then he would only take one person at home in his car and constantly try and convince himself that there was only one good choice and that he had gotten the most out of the situation. "I couldn't help everyone so I had to pick one". This is not right.

From our early kindergarten days to our late college graduation days we are being trained and taught to focus on getting good test grades and not on thinking outside the box and using our brain in a more creative way to solve problems easier. We only care about the outcome but not the process which is far more important. This is not good. This is just being trained to use vertical thinking. Instead, we should teach ourselves to use the lateral method.

You must always question yourself before making any decision. Why am I doing this? What is the best way to do it? What will the outcome of my decision be? Do I truly want this? Why do I want this? What are all the pathways that I can create? What are all the options that I can combine together in order to bring the best out of my current situation?

Understanding why you truly want something will make it easier for you to **create** the best way to do it and that will usually be something that is "outside of the box".

Some people just don't want to accept lateral thinking as a valid thinking method because it makes them feel like it threatens the validity of the more famous vertical thinking method. This is not the point of lateral thinking at all. Both of the processes are complementary, not antagonistic. Lateral thinking is very useful for generating ideas, creating different pathways and solutions or approaches, and vertical thinking is useful for developing them. Wise people would use lateral thinking to enhance and increase the effectiveness of their vertical thinking method by offering it more options to select from. Vertical thinking, on the other hand, will multiply the effectiveness of their lateral thinking method by making good a very good use of the ideas generated by it.

Most of the time a person might be using vertical thinking but when a situation calls for lateral thinking he needs to understand that no excellence in vertical thinking will solve the problem. To keep trying and persisting with vertical thinking in a situation that needs lateral thinking can be dangerous and lead to very bad decision making that might impact one's life. A wise person would be skilled in both thinking methods, and a master thinker would be able to combine them both in order to get the best out of the two worlds.

Here's a good example that might help you understand it visually. Imagine a car. That car has a reverse gear. You simply cannot drive the car in reverse gear all the time because that's stupid.
On the other hand, you must have it and know how to use it because sometimes in your life you get stuck in a blind alley. Then you need to apply the reverse gear or in this case, the "Lateral thinking method" to get out of it.

Vertical and lateral thinking are not that much different. Both can be useful in a given situation. It's not about one way being so much more effective than the other. They are both necessary. It is a matter of being able to recognize the differences and advantages/disadvantages of both methods in order to be able to combine their use effectively.

Chapter 5: Why we must think differently?

People are creatures of habit. Every single day they wake up on the same side of their beds and put on the same type of clothes they wore yesterday, they usually cook up the same breakfast and sit in the exact same car, take the same routine to their school or workplace and when they finally get there they do the same chores just like every other day, all over and over again.

Imagine being very old and almost finished with your life. All you have left is your memories and stories which left a mark in your mind. When that moment comes, do you really think that you will feel satisfied and fulfilled if you spent your entire life doing what others did and trying to impress the people around you? I think not. You will be full of regret, grief and constantly blame yourself for not living the way you truly wanted. So you should wake up before it is too late. You might feel comfortable now because you have no challenges, nothing to stand up for and everyone is normal towards you because you're doing everything exactly like them, but being in your comfort zone does not always mean being happy. In fact, it almost never means that you're happy.

We have only one life and our time is ticking away. Can you think of a person that wasn't different but left a mark in history? I know I can't. If you are just like everyone else and just another sheep in the herd nobody will ever talk about you and you won't be interesting to no one.

You need to ask yourself if you are truly happy with your current state and the current place that you are in. Are you getting the best out of your life? Are you truly living the way you want? Is there something that you're not doing just because you think that everyone else would laugh at you or think you're weird because of it?

Have you been taking any challenges lately? Are you "daring

greatly"? Or are you just living like a timid soul who does not know about a victory or a defeat?

Something has to change if you are not happy. Life is a wonderful journey full of great and exciting stories and experiences. You can't let yourself live like a bird in a cage. Spread your wings and fly far away. Stop worrying about what others think. Leave the TV alone, you don't need it. Stop wasting time on social media, go out and meet new people. Expand your horizons. Listen to your heart.

Stop fearing failure. Many people want to do something, but they are just so afraid that they are going to fail at it that they don't even attempt doing it. One of the key problems here also comes from our childhood. The fear of failure almost always comes from the early age when we get the destructive criticism from our parents for failing at something. Some people who suffer from this simply get paralyzed when they are offered an opportunity to do something different and exciting in their life. They will just give up on it before even trying and then spend many hours and sleepless nights convincing themselves that it was a good decision and they wouldn't have made it anyway even if they tried. It is hard to change something that has been carved into our heads from a very young age, but it is not impossible. We need to train our minds to look at the rewards and positive experiences that we will get out of the situation, even if we somehow manage to fail. Failures are nothing but lessons in life. And they are the most valuable ones. Nothing is a better teacher than a failure.
Take a look at this example of poor and wealthy people.
Rich people always try and manage to find a way to create more value, to produce and develop services and products that will enhance and enrich the lives and work of many people. Rich people almost always tend to put in tons of effort before they take out. They don't believe in something called "easy money" or getting something for free or nothing. They believe that you must work, earn and pay for what you're getting. On the other hand, poor people lack this type of understanding and they only see an option of putting as little effort as possible to get as much out of the situation as they can. They are always out trying to get something for free or for as little as possible. They all want success without effort, getting riches without

labor, getting money out of the sky with no effort and achieving fame without possessing any talent. They gamble, buy tickets for the lottery, go to their workplaces in the last possible minute, waste their time while they are there trying to do anything else but working and then leave in the first minute possible. They waste their money, time and energy on methods that are supposed to bring them wealth or fame without any effort, not realizing that all of that time can be used to improve themselves as people and increase their skill in doing something that is actually worth doing. Lining up by thousands of people for auditions such as American idol without even having elementary talent and skill to participate will bring you nothing but disappointment and wasted time.
One of the biggest secrets to becoming wealthy and successful is to always give your maximum no matter how much you are being paid. If you always tend to do this, the universe will simply find a way to put you in the place that you deserve, someone will recognize your skill and talent and take you to a better place where you can truly show up your work for what it's worth.

Always make sure to go the extra mile. Always tend to put in far more than you're willing to take.
In my experience, poor people tend to use the vertical thinking method only without combining it with all the pathways that lateral thinking can open up for them. They always tend to exclude one out of two options and go with the one that seems better for them at the moment instead of combining every other detail in order to get the best out of the situation that they're in.

And it not just about being wealthy or poor. Giving our best in every single situation of our lives will help us be the better person that we all want to be. It does not necessarily mean that it can only be applied in school or at your workplace. Any activity that you do always gives your best to do it with maximum effort. People will appreciate you a lot more.

In this chapter, I will talk to you about Risk management and the fear that some people have when it comes to making a certain decision.

Some people are not fully using their thinking abilities and the entire capacity of their mind, simply because of the conditioning that they went through while they were growing up, which made them have this fear mentality. I will list some of the reasons why people are afraid to think differently.

For example, in the middle (dark) age, people that had different thoughts about religion or anything else were considered heretics or witches and they were burned alive, beaten or stoned to death. Even great minds such as Galileo Galilei were "bullied" in some way for thinking differently.

Thinking almost always brings somewhat of a change. And people are afraid of changes.

Thinking deeply about something can uncover some deeply buried memories, questions about life, make us reconsider our way of living or make us realize that we're doing something wrong but we're so deep into our comfort zones that we got used to it. Even though changes are a necessary part of our spiritual growth, some people are really afraid of them.

If you don't allow some space for changes in your life, you will stop growing spiritually. And if you stop growing spiritually you will be very unhappy with who you are and always feel like you're lost and alone. And although you maybe will feel safe and secure by never taking or accepting any challenges or risks, you will always be filled with regrets for not daring to grab some of the chances or opportunities that life gave you.

A lot of people simply choose to be ignorant, they are afraid that by thinking they will ruin their lives. For example, some people that are very religious just because someone else told them to be, are afraid of thinking about it because they might start questioning their beliefs and the entire religion. This might be a silly example but trust me, I know people who are afraid to question their religion and beliefs because they think when the time comes they will be sent to hell for doing it, so they just keep pretending that everything they heard or read about it is true without even trying to understand it. Ignorance is bliss.

Thinking can make us aware of some problems that are currently a part of our lives and urge us to find solutions for them. For some people, such realizations can be sometimes very painful and hard to swallow. This makes them not want to face their problems and just keep telling themselves that everything in their life is the way it should be.

Freedom and responsibility almost always go together in the same package. But, people hate taking responsibilities so they don't embrace freedom. Ever since our young age, we learn to place the responsibilities to someone else's shoulders, blame others for certain situations and for the kind of life they're living, without ever criticizing ourselves. We tend to always comment about others but never about us. We never look at ourselves and our own mistakes that we make in each day of our lives. The number of times we lied to someone we love or said something that hurt somebody else. Taking a look at ourselves means that we will find many flaws because nobody in this world is perfect, and this will always bring responsibilities which people tend to hate so much. And what is the best and easiest way of avoiding such responsibilities? Stop thinking and let others think for us. Don't stress yourself and let somebody else do all of the dirty work for you. Just sit back and criticize others and comment on their flaws. Sadly this is what the majority of people do. This is also the reason why we give the power to politicians and other sorts of leaders. We believe that they can fix all of our problems and that they are the "savior". Nobody can save us from our flaws and the insecurities that each one of us has. We cannot run from our problems and responsibilities forever. They will eventually catch us, trust me, they really will. The only way to deal with this is to face yourself and start making a change. No problem can be solved by running far away from it. It can only become bigger and harder to deal with when the time comes. And the time always comes.

We always think that if someone else changes the world will be a better place, but we never try to change ourselves because we are so afraid and insecure, our egos are high yet fragile. Change starts from within. **Change starts with who you are. Be the change you want to see in this world.**
You need to understand that changes cannot happen overnight. You cannot change who you are in just a couple of hours or even days or months. You need to start improving step by step, each day is a new opportunity to be a better person. **Changes are good, we need changes. Everything around us changes as each second passes by.**

Let's take a look at some of the changes that are fun to do and usually help us discover new things about ourselves but also help us deal with problems more easily.

Travel

A wise person once said: "The world is a book, and those who do not travel can only read one page of it."

I'm sure we've all heard stories or watched a movie about a famous businessman who after years of work decides to sell everything he owns and just travel the world as much as he can. To be honest, this is not very rare anymore. People get obsessed with traveling more and more because slowly everybody is realizing its benefits. It is one of the best changes that you can make in your life. You meet new people and create beautiful memories of many different and wonderful places. Traveling is also proven to be one of the best cures for depression, anxiety, and narrow-mindedness. When people finally return to their homes after a long journey, they are simply not the same anymore. They are a better version of themselves. Even short trips have the same benefits and they can also serve as a starting point for people who are just getting into traveling. Traveling makes you explore different cultures and lifestyles that can often help you overcome some insecurity that you have about yourself for being different than the others. For example, you can meet people that have the same interests as you and you will feel much warmer and like a good fit when you're among those people that you share common ground with. It also makes you feel much better outside of your comfort zone. People who do not travel have a very small comfort zone and even going to the closest grocery store can feel like something intimidating to them. This also indirectly impacts your confidence levels. People who travel more are more confident than people who don't. A truly undeniable fact is that facing new experiences help people build confidence. Believe it or not, it can also impact your decision-making abilities and make you a better thinker. The ability to make certain decisions is important, yes, but imagine having to make decisions when you're alone in a foreign country. It is simply a very good practice that will help you become much better. Travelers also tend to utilize Lateral Thinking a lot. When you travel you only rely on yourself and the choices that you and only you make. This forces you to think outside of the box and make sure you get the best possible outcome out of every situation that you find yourself in during your journeys.

Traveling helps you learn your true self and find out things about you that you never really knew. This is one of the most important things and advantages that traveling can offer to a person. There is nothing better than fully knowing yourself.

Traveling alone gives you the opportunity to spend lots of time on your own, think about your past and future and it helps you clear your mind and gets a better angle of view for the current problems in your life that need solving. When you are really far away from your friends, family, and society that you see every single day, you can truly be honest with yourself. Sooner or later, we all have to find out who we really are and who we really want to be in life, and traveling will only enhance this experience for us.

For some people, it sometimes might be a bit harder to open up to a person and reveal their vulnerable and private things, but trust me, it helped me tremendously. I was a very anxious person myself and I kept things really private for a long time. When I first started openly talking to someone it was a random stranger in a bar and we both shared very powerful and valuable thoughts. I found out that he is exactly like me and that he just wanted someone to talk to. Many people are in this situation. Talking to anyone about your problems will really help you out. It can be a friend, a parent, a girlfriend or a complete stranger. After that I felt really good and like I had a huge rock fall out of my chest. The relief was incredible. This is when I finally realized that I should stop living in a cave and start communicating with others some more. You will be surprised how many people are also socially anxious and afraid to talk to someone not knowing that you both share similar if not exactly the same problems. Also, if you're a more confident person that is not really anxious about talking to others, one of the best things that you can do for someone if you see that they're going through a tough period is to simply ask them what's wrong and talk to them. It will mean a world of a difference to them and they will forever appreciate you. I cannot explain to you how many times I had a problem and I thought I was alone in it just so I go meet my friends and they tell me they have the exact same problem and suddenly everything is much easier. Sharing with others is really important, but also make sure to listen to other people's problem as well if they need someone to lean on.

Humility will make you the greatest person ever.

In today's world, everyone is pre-occupied with external looks, bragging about personal achievements, Instagram followers and what not. Everyone just wants to be at the center of attention and their biggest goals are getting rich and famous. People love being around a person that radiates humility because they know whatever they say is fully heard, they are fully seen and accepted for who they are by that person. That person just makes everyone feel better, so others value his/her presence a lot and consider it as a gift. People like these also tend to see life as a school, they know that nobody of us is perfect and they are always improving themselves through accepting constructive criticism and advice from others. They are open to new ideas and utilize them in ways that help them improve in every field. They accept their mistakes and are not stubborn when it comes to admitting when they've done something wrong. This takes us right into our next chapter dedicated to making mistakes and how to live with them.

Chapter 7: Understanding that you cannot always be right.

To some, admitting their mistakes is not easy at all, but this is a very crucial step when it comes to becoming a better person and an overall better thinker.

Learn from your mistakes and the mistakes of others. Study about other people's situations where they made a mistake and when it really made an impact in their lives. Think about different scenarios that you might find yourself in one day.

Remember, you can only learn from a mistake after you admit that you made it. If you're the type of person who instantly starts blaming others or even the entire universe for your own mistakes, you will never be able to utilize them as lessons in life. But, if you are bravely stand up and admit to yourself "This is my own mistake and my own responsibility" the chances of learning something and becoming a better person will be drastically increased. Since early school days, we're taught to feel guilty about failure and to do literally anything we can to avoid mistakes. Some kids are even taught to cheat on tests or exams just so that they won't get a bad grade and ruin their parent's reputation. This creates very bad habits and will later translate into a very bad person and low qualities as a person. The sense of shame, fear of mistakes and yet another failure is what keeps many people away from goals and success.

Don't just admit in front of other people for the sake of admitting or so that you won't be considered ignorant. Truly admit it to yourself that you made it, and accept it. Every time you admit that you did a mistake you become a better person and you grow even more spiritually. Understand that you are not in control of this universe and that you don't know everything that's going on. Sometimes you are simply not right in an argument. Admit it. Don't force your own opinion on others.

Be wise. Don't just try to run away from the possible blame you might be getting. Don't try to blame someone else. Everybody makes mistakes. Admit.

Here's what it takes to be able to learn from your own mistakes:

People who admit when they make a mistake are usually almost instantly forgiven and people have respect for them. The ones who never admit and keep running from them or blame others are usually the ones that nobody enjoys being around.

For example, if a friend tells you that you are always being stubborn in an argument, even when you are not necessarily right, instead of starting another pointless argument with him as well, you need to take this advice and really think about it. If you really know that this is true, you need to be brave and consider making a change. I know a lot of people that simply always want to be right, even when they are not. People don't enjoy being around an ignorant and stubborn person. Don't be that guy.

This is a method that I use and it really helped me a lot. **Create interesting situations and scenarios in your head** where you can make a mistake or where you've already made one, and work from there. Try to fully visualize and understand the situation and using the lateral thinking method that I talked about earlier, try to combine all of the pathways in order to create the best possible outcome from the situation. Practice this often and you will soon find out that you are able to deal with situations much easier, and instead of blaming others for your mistakes, you will simply not make them anymore.

I know that each one of us has an Inner Compass built inside that provides us with guidance about what is the best way forward for us. But the question that everyone wants to know the answer to is how does it actually do this? How does it guide us? The simple answer is that it goes through our emotions. They are the most powerful thing that we possess. Let's take a closer look at this.

Everyone knows when something feels good or bad, everyone knows the difference between feeling angry and feeling love, between feeling depressed and feeling joyful... but what most of us don't understand or realize is that these emotions are important indicators because they are giving us vital information about what is going on in our lives.

When you stop and notice what's going on inside you, you will see you are probably experiencing a wide range of emotions, emotions which vary depending on the situation you are in. Whether it's what's going on in your family or what's happening as you interact with your partner or your colleagues at work. But it docs not matter if we are aware of this mechanism or not, our emotions are still there and they exist. All of the time. This means that even if we like it or not, every single one of us has an inner compass that will keep providing us with this information through our emotions.

Live in harmony, fully understand, accept and embrace who you are.

So when you and what you are thinking and doing are in alignment with who you really are and what's best for you, you are in harmony with who you really are. Which translates into a feeling of joy, flow, ease, and happiness because you are living in alignment with your true nature, your deeper essence, or you could say with your soul essence. And then, the connection is open between you and the Great Universal Intelligence that is orchestrating the dance of Life. So Life feels good and is good and you are in flow – and things just seem to work out better for you.

When you're doing something that you don't really enjoy doing, you know it. Your mind and body will simply give you a signal that what you're doing is just not right for you. For example, if you prefer hanging out in the park with a more "alternative" type of people instead of going in the mainstream clubs and discos, spend your time where you prefer spending it more. It is your own life with your own rules and nobody can tell you what to do or where you should go. If some of your friends prefer going out and partying every day but you want to read a book instead, you should not force yourself to go with them. Yes, you might want to try it once or twice to see if you really like it, but if you find yourself sitting awkwardly in the middle of the club not talking to anyone and on top of that you hate the type of music playing in the background, why would you keep doing it? I agree that there are some things in life that we simply don't know if we like until we try them, but if you see that it is just not right for you after a couple attempts… Don't force anything. **Apply lateral thinking in these kinds of situations**

Listening to your heart

Learn to listen to your feelings and emotions. I think that each one of us is born with an ability to sense when something is "right" or "wrong" for us. We should not mistake this with letting only our emotions or animalistic behavior take over. Everything in moderation. We must not suppress our logic and reasoning. But, sometimes the heart is the one with the smarter decision. Since the beginning of our adolescence period, we are somehow "trained" of always finalizing a decision by using rationality and logic that our brain provides. Especially when we need to make a life-changing decision. But, not every decision brought by our brain is necessarily right. Logic and reason can sometimes fool us into believing that what we decided is best for us, which leaves our heart outvoted and left behind. Try to imagine the severe consequences when a person is supposed to change his workplace in order to get a bigger salary but the job requires him to go far away from home. Yes, the brain will make you bring a decision based on the current financial state but the heart knows that you simply don't want to leave your home and family and go work overboard. The heart does not care about getting more money or luxury, but it does care about your home, family and their good being and happiness.

The mind is capable of creating the most beautiful works of art, it serves as the source of scientific brilliance and an origin of inventive solutions to many complicated problems. But, it is also often caught up in the boundaries of the physical life and the drama and fear that surround us daily. When you're facing a problem, the mind will come up with a reasonable conclusion and this is why we're tempted to accept that one as the right one, but there is nothing more powerful than feeling a strong signal from your heart when it comes to making a certain decision, and we've all felt this before. Love, for example, is the strongest emotion that a human being can feel. And not just humans, animals feel love too. If you were in love before you know how it feels and how nothing can even compare to it. In fact, this emotion is so strong that even science cannot explain how in certain moments it can suppress all other also strong emotions like fear and such. For example when a mother lifted an entire car to save her baby that was trapped under it, or when a dog that loves his owner will fight against ten other dogs just to save him even when it clearly knows that he will lose the battle and most likely end up dying or getting injured really badly. This only shows us why love is the most powerful emotion, and we all know that it comes from the heart. So listen to your heart when it signals you.

Conclusion

Every morning when we wake up, we have a decision to make. Starting from a very simple one like: "Which shirt should I wear today?" or "Should I eat lunch now or after work?" to some more complex ones like accepting a different job that is abroad and such. But, the most important decision that we are supposed to make do we want to be a better version of ourselves today or not. Each day we are given a chance to make a significantly important change in this world. The only question is are we willing to take it. Every one of us lives a different life, filled with countless different stories and experiences, but we are all humans and we live on the same planet. We need to stop looking at races, colors, religions and anything else that is used to separate us from one another. We all face the same problems and each day we give our best to think our way out of them. We think just as much as we breathe, which obviously means that we should give as much effort to thinking as we do to breathing. I want everyone who is reading this book to understand that we are unique and we possess different qualities that we can use to make this world a better place.

We can help each other and we can use our minds in a much more positive way, not for destruction, creating wars and bringing tears to others. We are created and brought on this Earth to be much more than that. We have been given a magnificent brain capable of solving the most complex problems that we can imagine. Stop wasting time on social media, stop being worried about how you look and stop buying expensive clothes, you don't need them to look good. Positive energy is the only thing you need to attract others. Stop looking at that Instagram follower count, appreciate people for who they are, not for the number of likes they have on Facebook. Find someone to love, leave your comfort zone and enjoy life.

There is so much to explore and so many people to meet out there. Staring at your computer screen or your TV will never bring you any good memories or unforgettable experiences. Stop allowing the news or other propaganda to brainwash you and alter the way you think.

Don't be a part of the herd. Don't be a sheep. Everything that happens in life happens for a reason. And everything that happens can be either a good or a bad thing. And this depends on you. Only on you. Every situation can be considered a lesson. Every experience should be a gift. Look on the bright side of life. Positive attitude and strong spiritual mindset will make you far greater than you are and take you a long way. Believe in your dreams. Success can be achieved as long as you keep believing. You can do everything you want if you set your mind on it. Be brave, be strong, be smart and care for others. Radiate positive energy and good vibes, people will love being around you.

Be a good thinker, make great decisions and arguments but don't insist that you are always right in every situation. Learn from others, if someone has something to say let them say it, they maybe share tons of knowledge that they would like to share. You never know how wise someone really is if you don't let them talk. Find balance in everything. It's the key to living a good and happy life. You are the creator of your own destiny. Just like you should balance both thinking methods that I talked about in this book. Leave your insecurities behind, don't try to seek perfection in everything. Everyone has flaws. Don't be ashamed of them. Instead, try and work on them so that they become advantages instead of flaws. Turn the situation and current state into your own favor. Be yourself and people will enjoy being around you. I believe that there is a perfect match for everyone on this Earth, you just have to go out and meet them. And that does not happen in a comfort zone. Whenever you feel like you're alone in something, remember that there are countless of other people who feel exactly the same. If you need help ask for it. If you feel depressed or anxious just talk to someone. It will make you feel so much better. Humans are created to help each other. We all radiate energy that can be used for a good cause.

Stay safe and remember: Your mind is the ultimate creation capable of solving every puzzle, there is always a solution to the problem that you have, and the only thing that you need to do, is just keep searching until you find the missing piece.

I hope that this book helped everyone who read it. I hope that you understood and learned something from my previous experiences, situations, and examples. Remember to always stay strong and remain on your own path. We only have one life and time is ticking away, so use it wisely. A Kung-Fu master once said:

*"You are too concerned with what was and what will be. Yesterday is history, tomorrow is a mystery, but today is a gift. That is why it is called **the present**."*

The Power of Opportunity

Aware of All Wonderful Opportunities in Life

Chris Smythe

The Power of Opportunity

Copyright © 2018 by Chris Smythe

All Rights Reserved

Disclaimer:

No part of this publication may be reproduced or transmitted in any form or by any means,

 or transmitted electronically without direct written permission in writing from the author.

While all attempts have been made to verify the information provided in this publication,

 neither the author nor the publisher assumes any responsibility for errors, omissions, or

 misuse of the subject matter contained in this eBook.

This eBook is for entertainment purposes only, and the views expressed are those of the

 author alone, and should not be taken as expert instruction. The reader is responsible for

 their own actions.

Adherence to applicable laws and regulations, including international, federal, state, and local governing professional licensing business practices, advertising, and all other aspects

of doing business in the U.S.A, Canada or any other jurisdiction is the sole responsibility of

the purchaser or reader.

Content

Introduction

In a world flooded with competition, be it in finding the right life partner, right job or learning to have a sound connection with your family and finances, one can be stripped off opportunities. Yes, there are plenty of opportunities to go around but what if you are the unlucky one who is not getting them? Why should you sit there and sulk? Why should you be waiting for an opportunity to find you, when you can get up and actually create your own?

Gone are the days when you could depend on your luck and wait for opportunities to knock at your door. Life moves at a fast pace and sometimes there is no looking back to decisions taken in life. Wise people know and understand the importance of creating opportunities and through this book "The Power of Opportunity"; you will be provided with the knowledge that can help you master the art of creating opportunities. When you learn and make yourself capable of attracting the right people and energy, you open magical doors of opportunities for you and for others around you.

There are countless people out there, uninformed and unaware of the wonderful opportunities surrounding them every single day. Instead of recognizing and utilizing these opportunities, they end up heading in the wrong direction. This is due to the lack of awareness that they have and wrong attitude towards thinking that they cannot get anything better. When you do not make use of opportunities and cannot create them for yourself, you waste your time and energy with people, jobs and decisions that will do you no good in life.

So why should you be amongst the unlucky ones when you have the perfect chance to change your life? Why should you be the unhappy employee stuck with the same job for life? It is never too late to learn the importance of creating opportunities. Presented in this book are the best methods through which you can be an opportunity magnet. If you follow the guidance and understand the essence of keeping the right mental attitude, you will soon find yourself with wondrous opportunities that you never even imagined having.

Your Attitude Determines How Successful You Can Be

Not everyday is the same; every moment brings with it a fair share of happiness, joy, grief and sadness. Unfortunate as it may be, that is the number one rule of life. Waiting for happiness to knock at your door, or waiting for the tides of grief to subside, is not how it works. Struggle is the keyword here, if you want to achieve anything in life, or simply move on from a current state of mind, you need to buck up, hold your head up high and "strive" through thick and thin in life.

In order to reach anywhere in life, you need to develop the right attitude. You ask what is the right attitude? The right kind of attitude cannot be objectively determined; it can have various interpretations, depending on the situation at hand. It may simply mean going for a jog to clear your head or standing up for what you believe in, even when the winds are in the opposite direction.

If you want to weather any kind of storm in your life, you need to have the right attitude. The right attitude not only helps you focus and get out of a certain situation or predicament, it also helps you identify opportunities, which might open up doors to self-improvement and enhancement, if nothing else.

As they say, opportunity never knocks twice; try to make the most of your present; soak in each moment as it is and grab each opportunity that comes by. Live in the present; learn from your past and start preparing for your future, but also know that nothing in this world will last forever. Having said this, living in the moment does not imply that you become ignorant about your future. The right approach towards life, in general, is to be as proactive as possible and to foresee any changes or evolutions in the future.

Evolve as a Human Being

Develop the Right Attitude

Having elaborated upon the importance of developing the right attitude, it is crucial to identify the nature of the attitude. According to various optimists, adopting a positive outlook towards life is the right way to perceive life. If you are wondering how to inculcate positivity in your life, give the below a good read:

Happiness is a Choice

Engulfed in an ocean of troubles, sorrows and grief makes it increasingly hard for you to re-surface and acknowledge the existence of a lifeboat or an island, by the corner. This simply means that whenever you are depressed or troubled, you tend to ignore that tiny flicker of hope and fail to consider happiness as an option for you. This is where having a positive attitude would help you and make you realize that happiness is just around the corner. But only if you are ready to embrace it.

You need to find the good in the ugly, a light in the darkness and a rose in a bush of thorns. The process of treating happiness as a choice and then pursuing it is no piece of cake. It requires a tremendous amount of perseverance, self-resolve and most of all, the willingness to dust yourself up. However, you need to realize that happiness hardly ever comes as an uninvited guest. Just like everything else in life, you need to strive for happiness and, many a times, this struggle might turn out to be the most difficult of all.

Learn to Prioritize

Prioritizing your life, in terms of the most and least important tasks, not only gives you perspective, it encourages you to think positively. The outcome of prioritizing is always beneficial for you and the people around you. Thus, prioritize your life in the following way:

Reinstate Your Purpose

Time and again, you need to keep reminding yourself of your purpose in life. Years of pain and suffering might have blurred your sense of purpose, but you need to try to rekindle that flame. Try to redirect your life to a time when you truly felt happy and then reassess. Try to question yourself, what changed and why? Try to assess your situation and try to carve a way forward.

Identify Your Purpose

Having reflected upon your actions and words should give you sufficient food for thought to identify your sense of purpose. Start by prioritizing your responsibilities and see where your loyalties should lie, at work or at home. Chalk out a list of positive attributes you wish to develop with time and think of various ways to accomplish them.

Visualize Your Future

Form a clear picture of where you want to see yourself in the next 2 to 3 years. Hang on to that visual picture; if nothing else, it would motivate you to become what you aspire to be.

Look For Positivity Around You

Believe it or not, there is a speck of positivity even in the most negative and darkest of all situations. You might not be able to discover it with the naked eye; you need to use your inner eye to see beyond all the negativity. Faith and belief should be the two constants in your life and they will help you see the light at the end of the tunnel. Whatever happens in your life is a learning experience and take upon every hardship as a challenge, only to resurface as a survivor, stronger and more powerful than ever before.

Listen to Your Inner Voice

No matter how many motivational sessions you attend, unless you listen to your inner voice and talk to it, you will never develop the will to power through. Having said this, do not let your inner voice dominate you and try to reason with it.

Remove Negativity From Your Life

If you are trying to be positive, you cannot afford to surround yourself with negative people. They will simply discourage you and dampen your spirits. Moreover, try to rid yourself of negative thoughts, actions and things. The aim is to build a positive aura around yourself and not to let any unnecessary negativity seep through.

Looking at the Bright side

What is the bright side? Have you ever really given it a thought? Some people simply cannot acknowledge the greener side of the pasture, especially when they are buried under the rubble of troubles and sorrows. What they fail to understand is that the hope of a brighter side is going to help them survive and wage all of life's battles. Even when you see no light at the end of the tunnel, you need to believe that it exists and the only way you can get there is by being optimistic.

For those who have given up hope and are finding it extremely hard to get out of their current predicament, looking at the bright side is not at all easy. For such people, the following tips might come in handy:

Accept Life

The fundamental step towards a happy and contented life is to embrace life with open arms. Instead of whining over petty issues and your current state of affairs, learn to accept each facet of life, no matter how ugly or unpleasant it may be. Things just do not happen, the sooner you realize this, the better it will be for you. If you want to change your life, you need to take control and take the necessary steps to right all the wrongs. Always remember that time and tide waits for no one; your fate is in your hands.

Remind Yourself that You are Capable

At times, we don't know just how strong we are, unless being strong is the only option we are left with. You need to remind yourself, over and over again, that you are capable of dealing with whatever comes your way. Do not let your caste, profession or your relationships define who you are. Your inner potential is hidden and only you can truly exploit it, especially during times when you are tested. Ignore the voices around you and assess yourself, then only can you truly determine the power and strength you have within.

Disregard Others' Opinions

We spend too much time fussing over what others think about us. This only makes us weak and dependent on people and soon enough, we start looking at the world from other people's eyes. Always remember, you are who you want to be and you can never become a figment of someone else's opinions, unless you let them control your feelings and emotions. Analyze your inner strengths, weaknesses and disregard what other people think of you. At the end of the day, you are your best judge and the way you know yourself, no one else does.

Stop Comparing Yourself to Others

The brighter side of life will cease to exist for you, if you keep comparing yourself to others and complain about the blessings they have and you have been deprived of. If you have a habit of comparing, do it with someone who is less fortunate, so that you can count your bounties and become grateful. As for the voids you feel in your life, roll up your sleeves and strive to fill the gaps. What you need to believe is that your struggles, your faith and your capabilities are more than enough for you to strive through your life.

Love Yourself

At times, when your faith is shaken, you tend to bury yourself under a pile of complexes and try to hide from the world. You need to realize that you need to start loving yourself, before you can love others, be it people, your work or your external environment. Accept your weaknesses, bask in your qualities and try to love yourself, just the way you are. You need a reality check, every now and then, that whatever you are and whatever you have is enough to struggle through rough patches.

Keep Your Calm

Do not let others influence your behavior and no matter what they say or do, try to keep your calm, at all times. You do not want to find yourself in a situation where you end up acting irrationally, due to a nasty or ugly remark from a friend or family member. Always remember, you have everything at stake, you have everything to lose, not the other person. Therefore, be mindful of your behavior because, at the end of the day, you are the only one responsible for it.

Treat Life as a Journey

Do not yearn for the perfect destination in your life. Your entire life is a journey and it needs to be undertaken, one step at a time. Accept whatever life offers you and make the most of this journey, even if things do not work out the way you want them to. They never do, do they? Try to live in the moment, knowing that nothing lasts forever. This will make you appreciate the little things in life and give you the strength to tackle obstacles along the way.

Share Happiness

Share happiness and it will multiply. Ever heard this phrase? It is not only restricted to books of philosophy; it has a deeper meaning in life. Try to develop a positive outlook towards life and share that positivity with people around you. The aim is to share happiness and inculcate a feeling of mutual sharing and appreciation between your friends, family and colleagues.

Keep the aforementioned tips in mind and try to implement them in your life, regardless of whether you are weathering a storm or contented with your life. Positivity doesn't develop overnight; it takes considerable time and patience to look at the brighter side and to maintain that outlook, even during hardships and difficulties.

Always remember that life does not stay the same, all the time. Change is the only constant in life and the sooner you learn to be positive, the easier it would be for you to embrace the bitter reality of life. A little patience, perseverance and faith would go a long way. Rest assured, being an optimist would surely pay off, if not now, then in the long run.

Step Out of Your Comfort Zone

In order to achieve anything worthwhile in life, you need to make an effort; there is nothing like a "free lunch" in life. Yes, good things come to those who wait, but opportunities do not knock on those doors, where people are too comfortable with their current way of living.

The first and foremost rule of accomplishment is to step out of your comfort zone, do things which you never thought you were capable of, say things which were never said before and tackle obstacles along the way. You cannot expect your fate to do marvels for you, without even twitching a single muscle and making the tiniest bit of effort. If you are truly determined to achieve something, make that your aim or goal and give it all you have got.

If nothing else, stepping out of your comfort zone would expose you to a different facet of life and will enrich you with such a learning experience, the likes of which cannot be found in textbooks or motivational lectures. Life is surely a gamble, you need to play your cards wisely and always remember that risk and certainty is part and parcel of the game.

If you are wondering how to step out of the safety shell that you have built around yourself, here are a few helpful tips:

Embark on a Different Journey

If you truly want to step out of your comfort zone, try doing something different and ambitious. Until now, you might be used to doing activities and tasks, which were aligned to your personality. This puts a cap on the nature and type of experiences that you are exposed to. Try to do something which contradicts your personality and is a little demanding, so that you can experience something new and exciting. You never know, you might end up surprising yourself or the people around you.

Embrace Your Fears

The fear of a bad outcome or the fear of failure usually stops people from stepping out of their comfort zones and striving to accomplish something meaningful in life. If you want to approach a certain loved one and express your feelings, the fear of rejection and being let down might stop you from entering the battlefield, with your head held up high. You need to face your deepest and darkest fears and embrace them, as a part of life. Failure to do so would impair your ability to bring about significant changes in your life.

Many people have such strong fears that it becomes next to impossible for them to overcome them. Having said that, this process cannot be completed overnight, it takes a lot of time and dedication. The trick is to take one-step at a time and let yourself get used to the fractional changes, instead of drastic ones.

Involve People

Before embarking upon a new journey, involve a friend or loved one. You would be surprised to find out how much that would help. Having someone by your side, one who is facing the exact same things that you are, is soothing and comforting, at the end of the day. However, if your journey is all about self-exploration and self-assessment, involving a third person would fail to do the trick. Several journeys are meant to be embarked alone, so that you can truly capture the essence of the experiences you face along the way.

Make New Friends

Many a times, when you are desperate to step out of your comfort zone, the best way is to stop hanging out with your current group of friends. Try befriending someone, with diverse interest and hobbies and you will see a noticeable change in your thoughts and actions. A person's company plays a vital role in his/her personality development and what better way to change your perspective towards life, than to make a new friend.

Think of Positive Memories

Stepping out of your comfort zone usually means focusing on the positives and ignoring the negative voices inside your head. Before delving into something completely new and different, think of the last time you stepped out of your comfort zone and try to relive the positive memories of that specific incident. Negative thoughts would automatically perturb you and would distract you from your main goal and/or purpose. Do not let them get in the way of trying out something different. Adopting a tunnel vision approach would probably work best here. Therefore, eyes should be on the prize and the only way you can get hold of the prize is by thinking positive.

Do Your Homework

Sometimes your imagination becomes your worst enemy and tries to paint a gruesome picture of whatever you are delving into. Being double minded is completely natural, but you need to exercise a bit of self-control over your thoughts. Try to do a bit of research on whatever it is that you want to try and experiment. Try to track down various other people who have embarked upon the same path and gauge their experiences, thoughts and reactions. Rest assured, a positive word of mouth would benefit you greatly.

Other Techniques

Stepping out of your bed of roses always requires a high level of control of the mind, over your body. In order to reach such a level of control, you need to soothe your emotional state of mind. You need to have faith; you need to believe in yourself and your inner capabilities. The following might help you stabilize your emotional state of being:

- Use your imagination to your own advantage and try to let it wander in a positive manner. Try to form a rosy picture of how exciting and thrilling it would be to try something new and different.

- Food for thought is as important as food for the soul. Music is the most effective way to lift your spirits and helps you gain perspective.

- Practice a few breathing exercises on a daily basis, you would be surprised to find out just how effective they are.

- It's also helpful to take meditation classes and learn the various arts of meditation, yoga being the most popular one.

Five Ways to Be More Proactive

Do you know what it's like to be proactive? Have you ever given this nine letter word some thought? There is a popular misconception that being proactive is strictly restricted to taking an initiative and making an effort. However, a proactive person plans our each action, every step of the way and takes full accountability and responsibility of the decisions he/she makes along the way.

It is a shining attribute of a proactive person, not to play the blame game and to handle all the success and failures that come along. A proactive person knows that failure is not an end, it is a means to an end and it only helps you realize your mistakes and prevents you from repeating them in the future. Being proactive gives you a renewed sense of purpose and teaches you not to blame anyone else for your actions and decisions. Life in general, and the various challenges along the way, become easier and manageable once you become proactive. If you want to become a proactive person, it is never too late to learn; follow the five essential ways listed below.

Prioritize Your Life

The most important step towards being proactive is to prioritize your life, each and every step of the way. You need to list down your roles and responsibilities, in order and evaluate the relative significance of each in your life. Try to strike a work/life balance and take into account your most valued relationships. Prioritizing your everyday tasks and relationships would, in other words, help you allocate your time and attention, ranging from the most to the least important task on your to-do list.

However, priorities tend to change over time and you need to accommodate them in your everyday life. For many people, their family is the top most priority and for good reason. However, as your life changes, your priorities tend to change and you need to be flexible enough to make room for new people or responsibilities in your life's equation. It is advisable to schedule your life around your priorities, in order to do justice to yourself, your work and the people related to you.

Make Your To-Do List

Make it a habit, before sleeping every night, to draft your to-do list. If nothing, it will certainly give you a sense of purpose and direction. Chalk out all the activities, be if personal or work-related and write down their respective deadlines. Closely twined with the above point, making a to-do list makes you prioritize your life in a better and more efficient manner. A to-do list is practically a graphical representation of your mind map and lays down what needs to be done and when.

From a psychological perspective, it helps you plan for the near future, in a more constructive manner and helps you predict black swans along the way. What are black swans? They are giant, winged creatures, but not according to the current context. In truly marketing terms, black swans are referred to as events which cannot be predicted in the future and are outliers to the individual or business. The only way one can truly avoid them is by being proactive and planning out every single detail of his/her life.

State Your Outcomes

Failing to plan is planning to fail, right? This might sound as a cliché but has a profound meaning, especially when it comes to being proactive. An inherent part of planning is the process of objective and goal setting. After prioritizing your life and making a to-do list, you need to be clear about your goals and ambitions.

Ask yourself, what is it that you are trying to accomplish? How would you want to see yourself, say at the end of this week or month? Even if your priority is to join the gym and lose a few pounds, your outcome at the start and end of the time period should be clear and well defined. Try linking your objectives to your priorities and accomplish each, in the order of their relative importance. Paint a mental picture and try to use your imagination, in order to successfully define and implement your goals.

Determine High Payoff Activities

Setting your outcomes is always the toughest task and once you have established clear-cut objectives according to your priorities, you are now ready to start with the screening process. Assess each activity on your to-do list and question its importance and role in achieving the respective outcome. Tasks with greater importance and relevance should be included, whereas redundant ones should be crossed off your list.

After identifying your high payoff activities, you should focus on allotting a specific date and time to them, so that you do not end up doing something else in that time slot. Again, your high payoffs are dependent upon your priorities; the greater priority a task has, the higher would be the payoff.

Share Your Plans

The last step in being proactive is to share your plans with people- not everyone, only the ones you truly trust. It can be your spouse, your manager or even your boss. This is the time to reflect upon whatever you have worked for in the past week or month. Give them the accountability to question you on your daily or weekly progress, so that you can reflect on your actions and gauge the relative success or failure of your proactive behavior. Try to identify points of weaknesses and loopholes in the plans and take necessary steps to rectify them in the future.

After discussing the five most crucial steps towards becoming a proactive individual, the relative importance of adopting this concept in your life should become clear. A proactive person is better able to deal with various unforeseen events, as opposed to a reactive person. A reactive person hardly plans and waits for the calamity to strike, before actually taking steps to rectify it. The choice is yours, at the end of the day: if you want to be prepared for the future, even to the slightest degree, being proactive is the way to be.

Extraordinary Life Plan

There are two types of people in life, the ones who occupy front row seats and watch their lives unravel, savoring the happy moments and reacting to the gloomy ones. Others, on the contrary, take charge of their lives, develop the script and try to control the events in their lives. The former are usually categorized under reactive, while the latter is grouped under proactive people.

Give it a thought; where can you classify yourself? Is your approach towards a reactive or a proactive life? Or better yet, what do you aspire to become? The choice is truly yours, but before you make a decision, you should be aware of the pros and cons of each.

For those who plan each and every detail of their lives and wish to take charge of it, a life plan comes in handy. What is a life plan? A life plan is, in simple words, a dream churner for various people. Everyone has the right to dream, but only a few fortunate ones have the willingness and ability to turn their dreams into a reality. A life plan helps you achieve just that, a direction and a way forward, so that you can embark on a journey of self-fulfillment and self-actualization.

Various critics often question the importance and the need for developing a life plan. These people usually belong to the school of thought, which believes that plans never work out and life has a sinister way of surprising us, at various points in time. What they fail to consider is that life plans are made for a person's need for obtaining a direction in life. Typically, life plans help an individual in three main ways. Life plans provide clarity, in terms of the nature of the route to take in life, they help you juggle between various spheres of your life and most importantly, they provide you with peace of mind. Knowing that you have a certain degree of control over your life is, at times, oddly comforting and reassuring, especially from a psychological perspective.

Develop A Positive Vision

Do you have a vision in life? It does not have to be an elaborate one; a simple mental picture would suffice. A vision is generally a visualization of where you would want to see yourself, say a few years down the road. A vision is an accumulation of various aspirations and dreams. In a nutshell, a vision is a preferred way of life. Nobody can stop you from dreaming, but that does not mean you become a day dreamer. Convert your dreams into visions and then give it all you have got to materialize it into reality.

Vision Board Sessions

One of the most creative and constructive ways to motivate yourself to accomplish your visions and goals is to create a 'vision board'. Have you ever heard about vision boards before? They are widely used for corporate and entrepreneurial purposes, but can serve to be extremely helpful in shaping your future. A vision board is a visual illustration of your experiences, achievements and aspirations. You can place it either at your work station, at home, or somewhere you can see it every day. A vision board acts as a constant reminder of your goals and ambitions and to urge you to accomplish them.

Is a Vision Board Session Effective?

Research reveals that approximately 90% of how our brain works is stored in the visual part of your memory. Think of it this way, if you are planning a vacation to the Bahamas, you are more likely to develop a mental picture of the beach and the sand. These visions are generally at the back end of our brains and a vision board helps to extract these images and refine them in a sequential manner. Since a vision board is so illustrative in nature, it often extracts visions from your subconscious mind. Try designing a vision board and, if you are lucky, you will discover long lost visions, which you once used to cherish.

How It Works?

A vision board session is not only about collecting magazines and pasting relevant images on a board. While cutting and pasting pictures, you should ask yourself of why you made a particular choice. This will provide you with the opportunity to voice out your visions, goals and ambitions and will further help you filter each of them, in order of their importance in your life. Meanwhile, you will also be able to identify the various obstacles, which have prevented you from achieving and fulfilling your aspirations.

Who are they For?

If you think that vision board sessions are only for creative and artistic people, you will be surprised with its results for even the most basic of things. Vision boards can be for anyone looking for a sense of purpose and direction in life. Vision boards are specifically useful when you are going through drastic changes in life and when your priorities alter, over time. It might also be a good idea to develop a vision board during the start of a new year, so that you can plan out your life, based on your new year's resolutions.

So, what are you waiting for? There is a plethora of vision board sessions being conducted, almost all over the world. Try to find out the nearest one and enroll yourself. However, if there aren't any classes being offered in your vicinity, there are various online sessions available. All you need to do is book them in advance. Tryout a session, chances are you will experience a renewed sense of clarity and purpose in your life. A vision board will not only help you focus on your destination, it would also help you figure out how to get there. Take life as a journey and its obstacles as challenges, you would be surprised to discover your inner strengths and capabilities. For what it's worth, a vision board can be a fun and exciting experience.

Prioritize

You cannot be the Jack of all traits in your life. Even when you feel that you are swamped with chores and activities, you need to realize that all tasks and responsibilities in your life cannot be positioned on the same tangent. Some are less important than others and need to be prioritized accordingly.

Prioritizing your life is never an easy task and it always involves opportunity cost. This simply means that you must learn to forgo certain tasks or elements such as time, cost or resources, in order to accomplish your goals and ambitions. With respect to prioritizing, follow the tips highlighted below:

Is Everything Equally Important?

The first and foremost question that you need to ask yourself is whether you think that everything is of equal and unrivaled significance. An effective way of answering this question is to ask the people involved and those who would be affected by this process. Be it your family, colleagues, subordinates or friends, you need to ask them if they need any help or if there is any work that needs to be completed on an urgent basis. If nothing, this would help you chalk out your calendar dates for the next week, to say the least.

Another crucial way to answer this question is to work back, towards your deadlines and assess the hours of work they require and prioritize them on the basis of due dates. This would provide you with a sense of direction and purpose. Tasks or projects which require the maximum amount of input from your end can be prioritized first on your to-do list, followed by the least important and demanding ones.

Organize Your Tasks

You cannot just randomly decide to perform a specific task every day, there needs to be a properly laid out guide or manual. For your own sake, you need to have a system of accountability and productivity in place; otherwise, you would end up either repeating tasks or skipping the important ones. For starters, try to make do with to-do lists and later on when you get the hand of it, progress to advanced methods such as Gnatt charts or Asana. However, make sure that you are comfortable with your current methods, or else you would hardly use them later on.

Follow the Triple Constraint Model

From a project management perspective, the triple constraint model would be of particular importance, not only for project managers, but also for anyone who wishes to prioritize their day-to-day activities. Envision an equilateral triangle, with the three sides denoting time, cost and scope. It is practically impossible to reach all three sides of the triangle- this is where opportunity cost kicks in. If you increase the time to perform a specific task, its cost and scope would naturally increase.

In order to effectively prioritize your tasks, you need to work around the triangle and try to find the optimal combination of the three elements. This can be quite a demanding and difficult task, but with practice you will eventually get the hang of it. Of course, a lot depends upon the situation at hand. If your task is time critical, you would probably focus more on getting it done in a timely manner, paying little or no heed to the cost and scope implications.

Delegate

As mentioned earlier, it is practically impossible for you to perform everything. Therefore, delegation is often referred to as the essence of prioritizing. You need to delegate the slightly less significant or pressing tasks to co-workers, subordinates or even friendly, who are willing to help. Delegation is crucial for your project or task's success or failure, since it allows you to focus on the more demanding and pressing issues in your life.

Challenge Yourself

Assess your life, try to analyze it's worth. Ask yourself, do you like the same, old monotonous way of life? Do you want to do something to make it better? Or are you too afraid to step out of your comfort zone and try to bring a change in your life?

Challenging yourself every step of the way, is the single most effective way to bring about necessary changes in your life, don't you agree? Life is a challenge in itself and if you truly want to get out of the web of the same, old obligations and responsibilities, just step out of your cocoon and embrace life for whatever it has to offer. Whenever you are faced with a challenge, do not shy away from it, follow the tips listed below to make the most out of it.

Stop Shrinking

Various challenges come and go. Some people embrace them with their head held up high, while others simply choose to shirk their roles and responsibilities, until the calamity gets washed away. Instead of meekly entering the storm, enter it head first, all the while, preparing yourself for the worst-case scenario. You should know that life has a bitter and ugly side and the sooner you accept and acknowledge that fact, the better it would be for you.

Fight Fear

Fear is the most natural emotion your body can ever feel, especially during challenging times. Running away from fear would simply multiply it, embracing it with open arms would help subside it. Fear usually acts as a signaling mechanism and warns your body of the danger that lies ahead. However, what you need to realize is that, sometimes, all it takes is a major breakdown, for a breakthrough to occur. Always remember, fear would always be there, there will come a point when opportunities will cease to exist.

Remember Your Accomplishments

Your achievements and accomplishments shouldn't just be in the shape of a medal or trophy, forgotten on the shelf. They should be a constant reminder of the various challenges you faced and the emotions you experienced during that journey. Try to remember how nervous and afraid you felt at the start of it, but also assess where it eventually got you. Take pride in your achievements and learn from your failures that is the true essence of life.

Avoid Over-thinking

It is not that you do not have the capabilities to tackle a challenge, it's only because of your attitude that you end up suffering. Many of you make the mistake of over-thinking and only see the daunting task that lies ahead. Your focus should be on breaking down the task into a series of achievable targets. The trick is to take one step at a time and deal with the obstacles that come your way, one at a time.

Learn From Your Mistakes

You know what's as real and sure as death? Failure. No matter how capable or successful you might be, at a certain point in your life, you will have to deal with failure. Many people take failure as a sign of discouragement and as an end, in itself. You will fall down, you are bound to stumble, but the greatness of a person lies in dusting himself up and standing up for what he truly believes in. At the end of the day, when you look back, failure should only be taken as a tool to learn from your past mistakes and prevent them in the future.

Limiting Beliefs VS Creating Opportunity

Belief. Hope. Faith. These are the three bold words, which are always easier said than done. It is said that beliefs alter a person's outlook towards life and in troubled water, when the world shows you a cold shoulder, faith is what determines whether or not you reach the shore.

What is faith? Faith is looking at the darkness and spotting a speck of light, faith is taking the plunge, not knowing whether or not you will splash in the water or fall flat on the ground. Faith is that little voice inside your head, one that urges you to move forward, leaving behind the demons of your past.

Having said that, some people have what it's called "limiting beliefs" and these people need a bit of extra push to take a life-altering plunge. There are quite a few limiting beliefs that actually prevent you from being positive:

Different People are Weird

When you are used to a certain way of things or certain types of people, accepting diversity not only becomes difficult, at times it becomes impossible. What you need to understand is that not everyone is alike and life, at the end of the day, is not perfect, in any sense. You need to develop a degree of acceptability, so that you can give them a chance, you never know they might present to you the opportunity of a lifetime.

People are either "good" or "evil"

Some of you either filter out people and place them on a pedestal, or they simply position them on the lowest levels of morality. This means that they only have two measuring criteria for people, good or evil. Life does not work that way, every individual has a flair of good and bad, the degree of each varies and in certain instances one outshines the other. You need to give people a fair chance and let them prove themselves, before making hasty generalizations and making poor judgement.

Thoughts are an Indicator

People with limiting beliefs are usually unhappy or pessimistic, which is why they are always consumed with negative thoughts. They take their thoughts at face value and do not stop to fight off their feelings and emotions. For example, if they are getting a sinking feeling about a particular decision in life, they would take that as a sign to abandon that particular endeavor.

Control Comes With Love

Negative people usually believe that when they love someone, they are automatically given the right to control them. On the contrary, true love does not really demand authority and control; it is based on the foundations of trust and loyalty.

Want for More and More

Chasing after money, power and status lead you nowhere and makes you lust for more and more. This constant chase often makes you greedy and robs you of your inner peace and happiness. This simply means that no matter what you accomplish, you can never be truly happy and satisfied and you will keep yearning for more, all your life.

All the Bad Things Happen To Me

If you think that all the bad things happen to you, you are surely a victim of self-pity. Self-pity is such an unsettling state of mind that it simply erodes away all traces of joy and happiness in your life. Therefore, even if an opportunity comes by, such a person will not realize it, amidst the cloud of negative thoughts.

Create Positive Energy

Believe it or not, all of us produce and emit energies or vibes; these determine our personalities and how we behave under various circumstances. The energies intrinsic to your personality are usually channelized and externalized by your thoughts, feelings and actions. These, in turn, affect the people around you in either a positive or negative manner.

Various kinds and types of energies are around us, how you interpret those energies varies entirely from person to person. In order to develop the right kind of attitude towards life, you need to create an aura of positive energy around you. If this doesn't help, try to surround yourself in a positive and elating environment so that the positive vibes can rub off on you.

Ways to Obtain Positive Energy

If you think positive energy represents rays of sunlight shining upon you, think again. Positive energy is nothing but a state of mind, it is how you interpret changes around you and translate them in your personality. If you wish to create positivity around you, try to make a list of things that make you feel good. Therefore, the meaning of positive energy is a subjective concept and differs from person to person. Categorically, the following things might help in flooding your life with positivity:

-Close proximity to nature

-Yoga

-Swimming

-Reading

-Maintaining a diary or journal

-A vacation

Tips and Tricks

Positivity cannot be bought off an auction; it takes considerable time and effort to build a sphere of positivity around you. However, the following might help you think and feel positively:

- As soon as you wake up, resolve to have a good day. A positive attitude really helps, especially if you develop one early in the morning. Always remember that only you have the power to turn things around and make them happen for you.

- There are plenty of soap operas out there; you do not want your life to become one, do you? You should manage your relationships and try to reduce the number of emotional encounters with your partner. At the end of the day, you don't want more emotional baggage.

- You need to understand that no family is perfect; each has its own set of differences and problems. The sooner you make peace with this idea, the better it would be for you. Embrace the shortcomings of each of your family members and try to work around them, if you truly want to be a source of positive energy.

- Embark on a journey of self-improvement and self-assessment. You can do this alone or ask a friend to accompany you. This journey can be as simple as taking a foreign language class together with your friend or spouse. Know that you are not alone; you have all the emotional support system you need. This would really help you appreciate people for the positive role they play in your life.

- Use your imagination and form a rosy picture of how you want to see yourself, later down the road. Visualizing a positive, future state of affairs would probably motivate you to convert that image into a reality.

- Everyone has their own set of issues in life. If you truly want to be the source of positivity for yourself and people around you, helping a friend in need is at times the best thing to do. Helping someone out in times of need would make you feel a lot better about yourself and will clear your head. You would be able to focus on solving your problems in a better and more effective manner.

Identify Blocks

Life is a never ending road, or so it seems but it is in no way a smooth and uninterrupted path. You will not cruise through this path all your life. Always remember that good things never come easily in life, you really need to put in all you've got.

Before you embark upon any journey, prepare yourself for various obstacles and blocks along the way. How you tackle these challenges truly depicts your inner strength and capabilities. These blocks are not always physical in nature; they usually come in the form of mental demons, ready to pounce from time to time. Broadly classified, almost everyone faces the following obstacles, at least once in their life:

Failure to Set Goals

Some people simply cannot set goals and targets in their life, which makes it difficult for them to reach a particular destination. Having nothing to achieve in the future is a serious mental block, especially when you lose focus and direction in life. Like it or not, you need to list down your goals, so that you have a way forward. If you are afraid of setting goals because you think you might not be able to achieve them, you need to realize that everything in life is a gamble, it is completely up to you, how you wish to play your cards.

Fear

If you think that fear is a multi-headed monster, standing in your way, preventing you to succeed in life, so be it. Imagine yourself as a dragon slayer, ready to look at fear in the eye and slash it in two. Fear is the most natural feeling you can feel, especially when you face obstacles along the way. The truest greatness of a person lies in embracing his fears and taking life as a challenge.

"Courage is not the absence of fear, but rather the judgment that something else is more important than fear." – Ambrose Redmoon

Demons of the Past

Everyone has emotional baggage from the past; some keep it hidden behind doors, while others simply act as if they do not exist. The most constructive way to deal with such demons is to face them and let them out of your system, for once and all. Holding onto your past would only stop you from moving forward and achieving success in life. The trick is to rid yourself of all the negativity of the past and make peace with what the future has to offer.

Distractions

During the course of your life, you will face many distractions, which might turn into obstacles if you get derailed from your original mission. Your eyes should be on the prize and any distractions that come your way should shortly be disregarded. Do not try to find comfort in unhealthy activities like smoking, drinking or drug consumption. Life might present many shortcuts to you, but always remember that opting for them might prove to be highly destructive for your future, dreams and ambitions.

Bad Company

A man is known by the company he seeks. If you surround yourself with negative people, you might never be able to achieve your goals in life.

Nothing can be as big a block along the way, as bad company. Your friends play a major role in shaping your thoughts, feelings and actions. If the people in your life are unsupportive of your beliefs and goals, you need to find the kind of people who believe in you. Emotional support is crucial and even an ounce of negativity from a loved one can act as a boulder on your path to self-fulfillment.

Worst-Case Scenario

When life gives you lemons, what should you do? Most people would say make lemonade but shouldn't you instead save them for rainy days? Either way, life will give you your fair share of troubles and sorrows. The question is, how are you going to deal with it? Will you face your troubles with your head held high or will you run for cover and wait until the storm abates? Research reveals that the best way to deal with your fears is to confront them. Know that you control your fears and it is not the other way around. The most proven method for doing so is to mentally form a picture in your head. Imagine the worst-case scenario that you could have to face in a situation that you fear.

When you come to terms with the worst possible thing that can happen to you, you automatically prepare yourself for whatever you are about to face. The worst-case scenario can be anything. It could be a modification of your past incidents or an imaginary or hypothetical situation that is created around the characters in your life. You learn to accept life as it is, for its bitterness and ugliness and consider it as a true test of your capabilities.

In other words, you take up life as a challenge. You are willing to put in all that it takes in order to come out as a survivor. Thinking of the worst-case scenario gives you a will to fight back, knowing that you have nothing to lose and realizing that you have gambled everything that is dear to you. In such a situation, fear becomes an ally, not an enemy. In return, you come to terms with the idea of conquering fear and fighting off your demons.

Health is Wealth

You've probably heard the common phrase that "Health is wealth". It's not just a phrase that mothers use to make their children eat. A healthy body really guarantees a healthy mind and does away from ailments such as stress, depression and gloominess. Primarily, health is of two kinds, physical health and mental health. Both kinds of health are intertwined with one another. Stated below are the benefits of each kind:

Physical Benefits

Being physically fit requires you to maintain a healthy and balanced diet, regular exercise and most importantly, a positive outlook towards life. If you can manage to do that, you can benefit from a plethora of various benefits. Better yet, if you adopt the above mentioned habits in your life from an early age, you can manage to fight off diseases such as cancer, high blood pressure, diabetes and high cholesterol issues. All of this eventually adds up to a more energetic and effervescent you. The more energetic you are, the more productive you will be in your life.

Mental Benefits

Mental health is equally, if not more, important to physical fitness. Rest assured, eating a healthy meal and exercising regularly can contribute towards a more relaxed and peaceful state of mind. Whenever you are stressed or feeling down, always remember that you need positive energy to pull yourself from your current state of mind. The energy is required by your body to enable you to fight off the negativities in your life.

You will barely get the strength and motivation to fight off your stress with an empty stomach or with insomnia kicking in your system. You need to bring about certain changes to your daily routine, from a health perspective. Start off by doubling your water intake and devoting a few minutes from your daily schedule towards quality time for yourself. Incorporate the use of exercise and you will notice your mental health significantly improve.

Design Your Ideal Workout

When you reach a certain point in life, where you seem to have achieved most of your major milestones, you start craving for mental peace. The struggle we call life, is an endless journey that promises everyone their shares of bitter and happy moments. You can either take the back seat and enjoy the show, or take control of your life and know that you are responsible for it.

However, all the struggles in your life are bound to break you down. The only way you can get back up on the horse is by keeping yourself motivated and refreshed, especially during rough patches. Various psychologists recommend regular workout routines for their patients suffering from depression or any kind of crisis in their lives. Being physically fit clears your perception and broadens your horizon, not to mention the clarity and focus it gives you.

Follow the steps listed below to help you design the ideal workout routine:

Set Goals

Before you get to it, you should develop realistic and achievable goals. Ask yourself, why do you want to work out? Is your goal to lose weight or simply to keep yourself occupied? It is better to be clear and precise in terms of establishing your goals. Focus on specific aspects of your body.-If you want to work out for relaxation purposes, start aerobics classes, followed by yoga. Moreover, you also need to define your current level before starting your workout routine. Your goals and routines would vary, depending on whether you are an amateur, intermediate or have progressed to the advanced level.

What is Your Workout Frequency?

Based on your routine and everyday tasks, make a workout plan and allot specific hours of the day for each type of workout. Depending on your goals, this would give you a fair idea of how much you would be required to work out. The trick is to create the perfect blend between your routine tasks and your workout sessions. If you want stability in your life, keep moderation in your tasks. You do not want an excess of each, balance is something you should strive for.

Hire an Instructor

If you are just a beginner, it is advisable for you to hire a workout instructor. The instructor can help in suggesting various exercises and techniques, which would be suitable for your current weight, age and goal. It is really important for you to lay out your weight training intensity, which would only help you manage the exact specifications regarding your workout routine.

Do Not Over Burden Yourself

Designing your ideal workout does not mean filling up the empty slots in your schedule with excessive workout routines. If you overburden yourself, you will lose the motivation for working out. Only opt for those exercises, which you can bear to do, not the ones that completely drain you off your energy.

Chalk Out a Diet Plan

Your ideal workout would be useless without a carefully drafted diet plan. Here is where your instructor would come in handy. Equipped with the right experience and knowledge, your instructor would be able to draft a well-integrated diet plan, one which would complement your daily workouts.

Eat Well, Eat Right

When beaten down by life, many people cope with it by starving themselves to death. What they do not realize, is the fact that not eating will not help them deal with the situation at hand, it will only worsen it.

On the contrary, some people adopt the opposite attitude towards coping with grief or stress. They start binge eating and find comfort in foods like chocolate, cheese or ice cream. This is a graver situation than the former because it exposes your body to illnesses such as obesity or other side effects of an ill-balanced diet.

After a depiction of two extreme situations, the importance of eating well and eating right should be clear. However, if you have any more doubts, give the following benefits of a healthy diet a good read:

Mood Lifter

It is a well acclaimed fact that adopting a healthy and balanced diet, coupled with regular exercise not only improves your physical well-being but does wonders to your mental state of mind. Research reveals that physical activity has a profound effect on your mental health and stimulates brain cells to act in a more productive manner. It works well for those people who are conscious about their physique and gives them self-confidence and a sudden boost in morale.

"Another healthy habit that leads to better mental health is making social connections. Whether it's volunteering, joining a club, or attending a movie, communal activities help improve mood and mental functioning by keeping the mind active and serotonin levels balanced", says the American Academy of Family Physicians.

Helps You Lose or Maintain Weight

Eating the right kind of food, in the right quantities, is what determines your physical and mental health. One of the perks of eating healthy is shedding off the excess weight around your belly or thighs. Soon enough, you will notice a reduction in your weight. You surely cannot attach a price to the happiness you get, when you manage to fit into your old jeans.

Gives Instant Energy

If you think that the best way to cope up with stress is to stuff your mouth with comfort food, you couldn't be more wrong. Junk food, especially that rich in sugar, sucks up the remaining energy in your body and leaves it in a state of fatigue. Eating fresh fruits and vegetables, containing a high amount of fiber is what gets you going and gives you instant energy.

Fights Off Diseases

You probably have no idea how much a balanced diet can help you fight off even the most life threatening of diseases. By incorporating the most essential proteins and carbohydrates in your diet, you can avoid diseases such as high blood pressure, cholesterol and various other medical ailments. Put your guard up and implement upon the phrase- "Prevention is better than cure".

Release Stress, Meditation for higher awareness

Stress is perhaps, the single most disastrous emotion one can ever feel. It literally gnaws you from the inside, devoids you of all positivity and leaves you hollow from within. Needless to say, stress is one bitter reality and life has its way of giving you its fair share of worries and miseries- there is no escaping that.

Having said that, there are various ways that can help you reduce, if not eliminate stress from your life:

Meditate

Make meditating a habit. Before or after a hectic and stressful day, devote a few minutes of your time to meditating. You will soon realize that it will do wonders for your mental, as well as physical state of being. You need not follow a lengthy meditation routine, all you need to do is close your eyes, rid your mind of all negative thoughts and keep repeating positive statements such as, "I can do this". The key is to divert all your attention and energies to thinking positive, so that you can power through.

"Research suggests that daily meditation may alter the brain's neural pathways, making you more resilient to stress," says psychologist Robbie Maller Hartman

Be Present

When life seems meaningless and the future seems a distant reality, hopelessness and helplessness engulf you. However, you can step out of it by simply focusing on your present. Treat the present as a gift from God and try to see his greatness in all the little things. While taking a walk, take a moment to appreciate the sunset or the sunrise. Let the cool breeze caress your face and allow yourself to soak into the moment.

Regular Breathing exercises

Stress, in various circumstances, is a major reason for different mental and physical illnesses. You should never let stress take over your life; instead, you should be the one to control your life. Every morning, practice some breathing exercises. All you have to do is close your eyes and inhale and exhale deeply. Do not expect a significant change overnight, give it a few days- you will notice how refreshed and exhilarated you feel at the start of each day.

"Deep breathing counters the effects of stress by slowing the heart rate and lowering blood pressure," psychologist Judith Tutin, PhD

Vent it Out

You probably don't know yet but sharing your troubles and worries with your loved ones does a world of good. Even if the world turns its back on you, there would be that certain someone you can truly count on. Try to reach out to the people you trust and be receptive towards their input. After having talked to someone that you trust, you will notice an improvement in the way you feel.

Focus on Your Body

You need to analyze the extent of the influence that your mind has over your body. A stressful person is never a healthy one, the sooner you realize, the better it would be for you. Therefore, what you need to do is re-examine your body, for changes or alterations, especially in the way each body part is functioning.

"Simply be aware of places you feel tight or loose without trying to change anything," Tutin says.

Professional Life

Life is a stage where people come and play their respective roles. Who knew Shakespeare could be so pragmatic about life in general? This simply means that a person's circumstances never remain the same. While he performs his role and lives up to his character, he also exits the stage soon afterwards.

Similarly, you cannot always be a child or a student. Life moves on and before you know it, you have stepped into a puddle that people call, "professional life." Professional life is probably the first official reminder that life is anything but a bed of roses. The struggles, obstacles and dilemmas you face in your professional life, define your role in this world and in the lives of others. At the end of the day, given that you learn from life's invaluable lessons, your professional life makes you stronger and more confident than ever. Professional life is not only about pursuing your career and making a name for yourself; it is about making the right decisions, taking risks and defining the future course of your life.

Learn New Skills

If you think that graduating from a top school, with top notch grades and a medal of excellence is enough to last you a lifetime, you couldn't be more mistaken. This does not mean that your education is not important; it simply means that one should continue his/her learning cycle throughout their lives. You can never be too old to learn; at least that is what the experts say.

When it comes to stepping into the professional world, you need to keep in mind that your resume needs constant modification in terms of your skills enhancement. There are probably a million others out there, with the same set of qualifications and grades. Amidst this clutter, what employers are looking for is something out of the box, something unique that enables you to stand out. When it comes to skills and capabilities, there exists two generic forms:

Hard Skills

Hard skills are those set of skills which are taught and learnt over time. A person isn't born with them and these skills include learning a new language or acquiring training in Six Sigma.

Learn a New Language

You know how rewarding it is to learn a new language? From a business perspective, you should be well versed in Chinese, French and English, if you haven't learned it yet that is. Rest assured, this might be an extremely valuable addition to your existing resume and might get you the job you never even dreamt of. If the scope of your work requires you to stay up-to-date with new technology, you can also learn a new programming language. Try to learn the ones that are currently in high demand, so that you have a diversified portfolio, one that singles you out from the rest of the candidates.

Six Sigma

Ever heard of the terms "continuous improvement?" Six Sigma is a Japanese concept, which focuses on teaching techniques aiming to improve the quality of operations and processes. If you have an accreditation of Six Sigma on your resume, it will definitely help you get you to the right places. Organizations especially send their staff for Six Sigma training- if you are already trained, you can get into various huge conglomerates.

Soft Skills

On the contrary, soft skills are more innate and relate to an individual's personality. A person can either be born with them or the skills can also be nurtured. These skills include interpersonal skills, communication skills or even personal skills like self-esteem and integrity. Through learning, these skills can also be transferred from one person to the other.

Interpersonal Skills

Interpersonal skills are perhaps the most critical and crucial skills, not to mention a must-have on your resume. You need to possess the necessary people-skills, in order to get into almost any profession. If you think you are an introvert and are reserved by nature, take up a few classes and brush up on your interpersonal skills. Do not just add this skill on your CV for the heck of it; train yourself to talk to people in a confident manner.

Management Skills

Whether you want to apply for a management position or not, you should be equipped with the relevant managerial skills. Every position, no matter how menial, requires you to take decisions, lead people and communicate with them. Management skills help you avail the basic qualifications that help towards a better management of work force. These skills can really help you excel in your professional life.

Organizational Skills

Again, an employer wants someone who has prior experience or knowledge of coordinating and organizing people, resources and projects. In today's competitive corporate environment, organizational skills are no longer optional, they are pretty much considered as mandatory.

Evaluate Your Goals

Goals, plans and ambitions, are these only words to you or do they really mean something? Have you ever set goals in your life? How did that work out for you? Setting goals and targets doesn't really turn out as expected for many people. This makes them wonder where they went wrong. If you think that setting goals alone is a guarantee for your success, you couldn't be more mistaken.

Yes, setting accurate and realistic goals is extremely significant but the process shouldn't end here. You need to go back and evaluate your goals every once in a while, to determine whether or not you are on the right track. You can evaluate your goals by implementing the following:

Measure the Intensity of Your Aim

Try to determine the intensity of your ambition. If you want to become a painter, ask yourself if it is temporary or are you truly determined to achieve it. Your goals should have sufficient long-term backing; otherwise, you would just be wasting time and effort. An extremely clever way of monitoring this is by reverting to your goals, after a specific period. If you feel the same intensity and a stronger urge to achieve it, you should devote all your time and effort towards it.

Make Them Concrete

Concrete goals do not have to be written on stone, they just need to be written in black and white. Write your goals on a piece of paper and stick the paper somewhere where you can see it every day. If you want to be really creative, draft a vision board and get creative. Cut out an image from a magazine or newspaper, one that closely represents your goal. If going to Istanbul for a vacation is your goal, cut out a picture of any monument and paste it on the board. A visual depiction is at times better than a written one. However, it is advisable for you to make them more flexible, so that you can tweak a few things here and there when required.

Test Them

Make sure your goals are measurable, if not in monetary than in non-monetary terms. Simply stating out a desire is hardly enough; you need to make an action plan. The only way to test your goals is to compare them to your original targets and measure your progress.

Inconsistency is Out of Question

While making a list of your goals, make sure one goal does not contradict another. For example, if you want to take a vacation and reduce your debt at the same time, there is bound to be a conflict of interest. Learn to prioritize your goals in order of preference and practicality.

See the Value in Others

"No man is an island". This applies to personal life but has greater implications when it comes to professional life. If you think that you can manage everything and take your company to heights of success, without any help whatsoever, that is definitely not the case.

If you want to make something of your career, you need to involve the people around you.. The captain alone cannot steer the ship, likewise you cannot take matters into your own hands. You need to learn to delegate tasks and above all, learn to rely on other people. This will help you see them in a different light and probably enable you to value them more. Collaboration is the key, especially in a workplace environment. If you want to master the art of collaboration, follow the steps below:

Clarify Expectations

When working in an organization, it is extremely important to lay out what is expected from everyone- be it your supervisor, co-worker or subordinate. Everyone should be aware of their roles and responsibilities along with their respective contribution in a project or task. There should be a reliable system of accountability and reporting, which would really help highlight the required expectations to achieve desired results.

Get Everyone on Board

If you are a project leader, you should make sure that all people in your team are on board and well aware of how things work. Essentially, everyone should work towards the desired goal or target. Never adopt a tunnel-vision attitude towards your project, make sure all team members are working towards the betterment of the project and have no hidden motives.

Be Honest

Confrontation is the first and foremost rule of collaborating with your coworkers and supervisors. If you have a problem with the way things are, confront them and be honest about your issues with them. By holding back, you are simply turning your back on your issues and not giving them a chance to be resolved.

Meet Regularly

If you want to collaborate with your people effectively, the key is to hold regular meetings. This would allow regular and timely progress updates and would also provide you with the opportunity to meet and discuss issues. Make sure the meeting time is used constructively and should not be for pointless jibber-jabber.

Work on Your Social Life

"All work and no play makes Jack a dull boy". Does this ring a bell? Having a career and indulging in your professional life does not mean you cut off all social relations. It is ideal to have a balance in your life and work your way around it.

Look at it this way, the more you interact with people, the greater your social circle will become. This can do wonders for you, if you know how to make the right connections.

Take Charge

Do not sulk around and wait for people to make plans. At times, all you need to do is take an initiative and approach someone. Plan a movie, dinner or even a date. You can even host a party or a game night and call all your friends over; you never know how exciting this might be. Do not let the fear of rejection come in the way of taking charge.

Try Something New

You know it's never too late to learn a new skill, or try something new. Try a new sport or join a club membership that will allow you to meet new people.. Interacting with new people is something that can be truly rewarding and can open up various avenues for you- in terms of varying opinions and perspectives.

Prioritize

Just because you have become too busy with your work or in your married life, doesn't mean you give your friends the back seat. Make it a point to call them or meet up with them, at least on weekends. Be it a brief meeting for a cup of coffee or a movie plan, spare some time and make sure it's worth it.

Do not Hesitate

Turning down and declining every other plan can really put off the other person. If you continue to do so, you will not be left with any friends. Even if you do not want to make new friends, at least try to retain the existing ones. All you need to do is say yes every once in a while.

Value People Around You

At times, we tend to take old friends for granted. It will not take much of your time or energy to call an old friend and check on him/her, would it? Meet up with old friends and dig up old memories, you don't know how refreshing that can turn out for you.

Relationship

Positive Vibe

Positive energy can do wonders in creating opportunities. Everyone likes to be around people who carry and give off positive energy. This is because positive energy is attractive and can surprisingly be contagious. Positive energy can really make a difference in your life. It can enhance your spirituality and improve your general and mental health. In return, it enables you to move faster towards success and helps you in polishing your relations with people.

Your energy is essential, not only for you but for all others around you. If you are having a bad day and you meet a person who's giving off positive energy, you'll be feeling good in no time! Positive energy can help you create opportunities whilst negative energy can actually destroy your chance of creating opportunities. Let's look at two examples of differences in energy and how they may affect a common situation

Imagine you get a call for an interview. You dress appropriately, have confidence and are mentally ready for the interview. You arrive for the interview and greet the interviewer with a smile on your face. You answer all questions with confidence and use your sense of humour (decent) wherever applicable. Chances are that you'll make the interviewer's day and he or she would want to select you, just because of the positive energy that helped liven and brighten up the intense situation.

Now imagine you arrive for the interview. You are appropriately dressed but are nervous and hence mentally not ready. The interviewer asks a range of questions but you are lacking in confidence and therefore you look in distress. Without knowing, you'll actually be giving off negative energy and it will affect the situation. This will only make the interviewer feel less keen in hiring you. Always remember that regardless of the situation, positive energy will always help.

People that are positive, naturally make others feel good around them. They give off positive vibes that make them warm, welcoming and appealing to others. Positive energy allows people to interact with you comfortably and hence, you are more likely to make new friends and relationships that can change your life for good! Always remember, life is full of ups and downs and sometimes you may be prone to depression. However, positive energy will help you fight any difficult situation and will help all others around you too.

Start being a little bit more positive today and you'll be surprised to see the positive changes in your interactions with people and vice versa. Eliminate the stress from your lives by thinking positively and being optimistic. Let go of the negative people in your life that are not helping you grow. These negative people can really affect your chances of having opportunities. Their pessimistic nature will always get in your way and will make you think negative too. Take inspiration from good books and spend time doing what you love. Enjoy life and you'll be giving off positive energy before you even know it.

Meet New People

Meeting new people is a wonderful and easy way through which opportunities can be created. The more people you know, the more your social circle starts to enhance and expand. New people in your life will help you grow, they may help you learn and see life from a different perspective. They may be wonderful positive energy carriers that can help you with better opportunities be it at work, in a relationship or in general. These new people may have the ability to change your life!

You may not even be aware but a new person around you may be carrying an opportunity that you can really make use of. What use is that opportunity that is being wasted because of your lack of good communication skills? This is where good people skills can really lend a hand. In order to be able to meet new people, you must start by focusing all of your energy to being positive. If negative thoughts are cluttering your mind, you will never be able to meet new people with ease.

So how can you stay positive? Simple! All you have to do is think positive and good thoughts. Keep a smile on your face and do not worry about the outcome of the meeting. When you are smiling, you will come across as friendly, therefore giving off positive energy. As a result, people will notice you and you will become more approachable and easy to get along with. Not worrying about the outcome will help you stay relaxed and will allow you to be yourself without any worries.

Search for new people in places of your interest. People that are present in your place of interest are more likely to get on with you since you share a common interest. If you are single, you have a chance of meeting your life partner here. On the other hand, you can also try new places and meet individuals who you share nothing in common with. This can help create opportunities. A sense of curiosity in something can actually help you learn and grow since you are likely to inquire more on the topic being discussed.

There may be somebody around you, who you want talk to but are not sure how to. The use of some good conversation starters can really get you going. You may want to simply compliment the person or kill the boredom with a brief introduction of yourself. If you are at an event, inquire about how they know the host and how they heard about the event. Depending on the situation and how you connect, you can ask about their occupation, family etc.

When meeting new people, always keep a smile but don't over-do it. You want to come across as warm, welcoming and respectful. Avoid distracting people that may be busy with a phone call or another activity since it can tend to make you look rude. When meeting new people, keep the conversation general and avoid going into too many personal details. You don't want to come across as nosy and make the other person feel uncomfortable. Once you have set the pace for the conversation, things will get easier and you'll actually start to enjoy knowing the new individual.

Quality People and Opportunities

Quality is a subjective term and hence there can be no one definition to define quality. However in people, quality can generally be described as having quality features that make people more attractive to you. These may be people that are successful and live happy lives and people that enjoy their work and know how to inspire others. It might even be people that are funny and good at making you smile. Being around people like this can help create opportunities for you like never before.

Interacting with people that appeal to you, are successful and have a lot of good knowledge to share can inspire you and make you see life from a new perspective. These people can help you in making wiser decisions in life and can hence be a reason for opportunities being created for you. The more quality people in your life that you interact with, the more opportunities created for you. Let's explain this with a general example:

Imagine you are single and looking for a life partner. Your ideal life partner would be somebody who appeals to you and shares similar interests. If you have a vast social circle of friends, you have a good chance of finding a life partner amongst them. People from your group of friends will always be easy to talk to and you can get to know more about them without coming across as intrusive. The more people you know, the more you will be talked to and talked about and hence you have a higher chance of being asked out.

However, as mentioned earlier, it is important to socialise with quality people. People that you find qualities in should be the ones that you are friends with. Quality people will naturally appeal to you and your chances of interaction will always be more. On the other hand, people that do not appeal to you should be avoided socialising with. Some people can be so negative that they can drastically affect your positive energy and well-being just by their presence.

You always want to interact with people that can help you grow and inspire you to be better and feel better about yourself. People who are appreciative and have a respect for others are wonderful individuals to be around. Whilst interacting with quality people can help your personal relationships, it can also help enhance your business relationships. If your business has a team of quality employees, you will attract other businesses to interact with you. In return, you polish your business image in the business world.

In order to create quality opportunities, you must always present yourself in a manner that is going to attract quality attention. Be kind, friendly as well as professional. It won't be long before you start to turn heads. If you hesitate when it comes to talking to new people, you can make use of some of the tips mentioned in the previous section of "meet new people". Only when you are able to interact with others comfortably, will you be able to make the most of the interaction.

You are the Sum of the 5 People Closest to You

There is a wonderful quote by the motivational speaker Jim Rohn that states, "You are the average of the five people you spend the most time with." When you look into what is actually being said, you will come across a powerful finding. The people in your life, the people that you spend most time with and who you are the closest to, have a great impact on your life. They ultimately influence the person that you will become. And they surely do! Who you spend time with can enhance you as well as bring you down.

Take your friends for instance, imagine a friend that is always whining and unhappy with their life, it will also affect your happiness and optimism towards life. On the other hand, if you are having a bad day, an inspiring and cheerful friend can cheer you up and inspire you to stay positive. It doesn't only apply to your friends and affecting your happiness. The people around you can also drastically affect your personal success thereby affecting the opportunities that you may have.

Regardless of your intelligence, talent, skills, background and ethnicity, your success will always be dependent on the people that you surround yourself with. Good people that have qualities that appeal to you will help you be a better person in general. Their personalities and ways of dealing with different situations can enhance your well-being and help you make wiser decisions. Therefore, it is important that you are aware of the people that you hang out and socialise with.

The notion is fairly simple, yet it can be overlooked most of the times. In order to analyse the people affecting your life, start by asking yourself a few questions. Who are the 5 people in your life that you spend most time with? They don't have to be exactly five in number. 3 to 5 people are fine. Analyse the hours spent with them. These 5 people may include family, co-workers, best friends and your life partner. Then you want to go into a few more details regarding this group of people.

Ask yourself who those people are in your life and how they are living their lives. Keep their career and success in mind. How are these people in terms of personality? Are they ambitious? Do they inspire you? If you end up getting more negative answers than positive, it is time that you analyse the affect that they are having on your life. The people should be able to enhance you and help you move towards your goals. If they are not helping you grown in anyway, should you really be around them for so long?

You can also think of the people in your life that have qualities of being inspiring, helpful and thereby creating opportunities for you. If these people are not in the list of the 5 people closest to you, maybe it's time that you include them in that list. Always remember that although the people closest to you will affect your life, you will also be known by the company that you keep. Hang out with the people that have qualities that you will want to be known for.

Conclusion

Creating opportunities is very important in life. You must create opportunities and not wait for them to find you. Creating opportunities not only helps in our personal relations, but also greatly assists in shaping our career and enhancing our well-being. Our success in life is greatly dependant on the opportunities that we have and hence we need to ensure that we can create them for ourselves.

The ability to create opportunities is an art that can be mastered, if you follow the guidelines given in this book. Simple alterations and enhancements in your day-to-day lives, letting go of limited thinking, stepping out of your comfort zone, challenging yourself, creating positive energy, learning new skills and interacting with new people can all help you move faster towards your goals.

Our relations with people have the ability to influence us in a powerful way. These relationships with people need to be right. Knowing the right people and interacting with them in the right manner, can do wonders for your life and can create opportunities for you that you never even imagined. These people can help you find the ideal life-partner and job to ensure that you are successful in life.

Since we all are unique in our own way, we need to strive for excellence in everything that we do. Why wait for opportunities? Making smarter decisions can enable opportunities to be magically created for you.

Thank you for reading "The Perception Transformation Collection". If you enjoyed this book, please take the time to share your thoughts and consider leaving a review, even if it's only a line or two; it would make all the difference and would be greatly appreciated.

Thank you   *Chris Smythe*